PRAISE FOR
FROM **HECTIC** TO **HEALTHY**

If you want to take the journey to a balanced life, then let Craig and Mary take you by the hand and guide you. They have pulled back the curtain on their lives to reveal what happens when life is lived in perpetual spin and, more importantly, what steps need to be taken to make it stop. They have given us a clear path to follow on the journey to the balanced life.

Reggie Joiner
President/CEO, Rethink

If you want to read a book that is real and will cause you to ask serious questions that need to be answered, *From Hectic to Healthy* is the book for you. Craig and Mary open up their lives to us and share how life can spin and get out of control. They don't leave us there, however, but in a powerful way share how God and others have helped them and can help us have a life that is real and pleasing to God. This book is a must-read for everyone, no matter where they may find themselves in life today.

Tom Lance
Senior Pastor, Grove Community Church

You will find here a lot of true life, gritty insights into the challenges of work-life balance. Craig and Mary share their struggles, shortcomings and relevant insights learned from their journey. They unmask the comfortable myth that simply knowing Jesus makes life easy. Their story will bring you hope and give you encouragement. I strongly recommend this book for couples before they tie the knot.

Dr. Vic Pentz
Senior Pastor, Peachtree Presbyterian Church

Craig and Mary have courageously allowed us an intimate look at their journey. They have allowed us to stare in the face of a life that spins out of control. You will be moved, convicted, challenged and encouraged, but most of all, you will find help and hope for a better way . . . a better life.

Lance Witt
Replenish Ministries

FROM
HECTIC
TO
HEALTHY

THE JOURNEY TO A BALANCED LIFE

CRAIG & MARY JUTILA

Regal

For more information and
special offers from Regal Books, email us at
subscribe@regalbooks.com

Published by Regal
From Gospel Light
Ventura, California, U.S.A.
www.regalbooks.com
Printed in the U.S.A.

Library of Congress Cataloging-in-Publication Data
Jutila, Craig, 1965-
From hectic to healthy : the journey to a balanced life / Craig and Mary Jutila.
p. cm.
ISBN 978-0-8307-6222-4 (hardcover)
1. Simplicity—Religious aspects—Christianity. 2. Work-life balance.
3. Quality of life. 4. Time management—Religious aspects—Christianity. 5. Families—Religious aspects—Christianity. I. Jutila, Mary. II. Title.
BV4647.S48J88 2012
248.4—dc23
2011053488

Rights for publishing this book outside the U.S.A. or in non-English languages
are administered by Gospel Light Worldwide, an international not-for-profit ministry. For additional information, please visit www.glww.org, email info@glww.org, or write to Gospel Light
Worldwide, 1957 Eastman Avenue, Ventura, CA 93003, U.S.A.

To order copies of this book and other Regal products in bulk quantities,
please contact us at 1-800-446-7735.

To our children
Cameron,
Alec and Karimy,
and Blake

You are the light of our life and the light of the world. We love you and believe in you. Our hope and our prayer is that you each live a life in proper balance and with the right spiritual perspective. You don't have to change the world, but you can make a difference by living a life filled with God's grace, love and mercy. We love you!

Blake, your life reminds us that this earth is not our final destination and our time here is limited. Not only do you live in heaven with Jesus, but you also live in our hearts forever. We can't wait to meet you when together we can see Jesus face to face.

CONTENTS

Section 3: **Setting PACE**

Section 4: **Continuing WALK**

FOREWORD

By Dr. Jim Mastellar

The curse of busyness is mentioned by many but dissected by few. There are even fewer who are willing to expose their own struggle and near demise to this curse, as the Jutilas have done. I commend their courage in being willing to be vulnerable. More than that, I commend the work they were willing to do in facing their struggles. God in His mercy confronted them, and especially Craig, with the destructive path he was on. And I believe God does that for each of us in our areas of need. But, we all must make that critical choice: Will we humble ourselves, face our brokenness and join God on a healing journey? Or, will we continue to make excuses, blame others and defend or deny our brokenness right into our own destruction?

Your journey, and mine, may not be identical to theirs, but there are points of commonality that will always allow us to learn from one another. My prayer is that you will be open to these points of connection with the story you are about to read. You may find some things here that frustrate or discourage you. You will certainly find reason for hope, for praise and for encouragement as you go forward in your own journey.

Going forward always involves effort and struggle. But be encouraged—it is worth it! God has "given us everything we need for living a godly life" (2 Pet. 1:3). The question again is: Will we avail ourselves of this help? Craig and Mary opened themselves to the support and challenge of others, to extended therapy, to books and to the humility of being honest with each other and with God. But finally and primarily, they opened themselves to the truth of God's Word and His healing love.

If I could wish for one thing for you as you read this book, it would be this: I pray that you would be willing to look deeply into your own soul and face honestly the brokenness that is yours. And that you would then look up to see a God who loves you, and look out and see people who love you just the way you are. Your true self! You don't need to hide; you don't need to prove anything; you don't need to impress anyone. It is okay to just be you. Let God do what He loves to do for those who are willing. He wants to love you, heal you and give you an abundant life. May this book be part of your journey toward wholeness.

Dr. Jim Mastellar
CEO, Center for Individual and Family Therapy

Dr. Jim Mastellar is a licensed marriage and family therapist and founder and CEO for the Center for Individual and Family Therapy. He received his master's degree from Dallas Theological Seminary and his doctor of ministry from Fuller Theological Seminary. Jim also served as a pastor for nine years and has served as director for CIFT for the last 20 years. His wisdom and unique insight help hurting families make life-changing decisions that restore life and hope to those who need it most.

PREFACE

If you are a well-balanced, life-giving, emotionally and spiritually healthy person who thrives daily without complaint or fault, you will probably use this book to balance out an uneven couch, or as a coaster for your coffee cup. But if you find yourself nodding in agreement as you read through these pages, you will find comfort in knowing you are not the only one living a life of burnout and spin. In fact, we have hundreds of written responses from conferences where we have spoken that indicate you are actually in the majority.

Perhaps you are like us. Mary and I could be described as a "type A" couple that not only enjoys work but also thrives on the adrenaline it provides. We are overworked (our choice), compassion-fatigued people, working more on and in our jobs than on ourselves, or our family. This describes me (Craig) more than Mary. Many books have been written on our chosen topic of moving from a hectic lifestyle to a healthy one, but this book is different. After we spent 18 months in counseling and received the emotionally stabilizing input of supportive friends, the wisdom of wise mentors and a large dose of humility, I was able to regain traction in my life and in my relationships with Mary and our children.

Mary and I wish this book had been born out of what we know rather than what we went through. It would have been easier and far less painful. But it was born from difficulty and a life lived out of balance in many ways. That's why you can take heart in what you read. Our sincerest hope is that our story will spur you to take action, give you comfort that *none* of us has it all together, and help you experience God's infinite love and forgiveness.

We realize that most books can either be a "good read" or a "tough read." Our prayer is that this book will be both—a good read because it's grounded in gritty experience and founded on God's unchanging Word; a tough read because you've realized your life is spinning out of control with no end or hope in sight.

You will notice that throughout this book there will be humorous stories right alongside the painful ones. That seems to be the way life is sometimes. And though this book is not an answer to every problem, nor is it a simple recipe for finding life balance—we wish there were such a thing—we sincerely hope and pray that the thoughts, questions and Scripture in this book will be life giving, encouraging and resonant to your soul.

What Mary and I want you to experience in the following pages are hope, help and understanding as you read how we came to the end, did a U-turn and then began walking together again down a much healthier path. No matter where you are in your hurried and hectic life, you have a chance to begin again. You can turn around and start over, even if you have been traveling down the wrong road for many years.

God is a God of second chances, third chances and more. He is able to restore you and your broken relationships. He desires for you to come close to Him and have a healthy relationship with Him and with others. He even wants to walk the road with you, directing you around the obstacles and indicating where to turn.

We aren't writing as a couple that has it all together, but we are speaking from hearts that have been renewed and restored. Because of God's grace, we have something to share with you that can help you live life to the full. It is our prayer that our story will encourage you and inspire you on your journey to a balanced life.

Craig and Mary

SECTION 1

UNDERSTANDING
SPIN

1

SEASONS

I am not what I ought to be, not what I want to be, not what I am going to be, but thankful that I am not what I used to be.

JOHN WOODEN

The Journey Begins

When I opened my wife's journal and saw the words "I hate my husband" penned in black ink, I knew that it was the end—perhaps the end of our life together. In many ways, it *was* over. I knew that if I were to continue down the same road, there would be no chance of reviving a relationship I had been suffocating for the past 15 years. My workaholic lifestyle, my emotional detachment from my family and my overcommitment to outside interests were creating distance between me and my wife, but I was somehow unaware of the severity of our marriage problems. The reality started to sink in when the words from my wife's journal jumped off the page and put their hands firmly around my throat.

The easy thing to do when life starts to crumble is to point a finger and blame others or circumstances. I know. I did that for many years. It wasn't until the end came that I woke up. I had reached the end of myself.

I found out that after digging a hole of relational neglect for 15 years, one can't simply put down the shovel and jump out of the hole. You need someone to throw you a rope and be willing to help pull you up. Here's what that looked like for me. First, I needed to be forgiven by my wife and my kids, and I needed God's grace and mercy for my past choices. Next, I needed to be accountable for my time and I needed to get emotional support to take one step at a time. Last but not least, I needed the power of the Holy Spirit, who brings hope and peace.

If you have been digging an unhealthy relationship hole for a while, it will take energy, time and patience to climb out, especially if your digging was not measured in days or weeks, but in months and years. Mary and I, through the help of a wise counselor, supportive friends and the passage of time, were able to climb out of that unhealthy hole and start digging and even planting in a much healthier spot. In fact, we are now seeing some healthy growth as a result.

The truth is, when a person is faced with the harsh reality of losing everything most important in life, he or she has to make a choice. When the end came for me, I learned that it is only after you are broken that you can be put back together again. The important things in my life that were hazy began to get focused and become crystal clear. I felt renewed passion, a desire to refocus my priorities and a refreshed spirit. Coming to the end of something is an opportunity to choose a new beginning.

Retracing Our Steps

At the beginning of a journey, especially life's journey, you must have a start-ing point and a plan. I (Craig) had neither. I had hopes, dreams and aspira-tions, but no plan. Well, no plan for my family. I had incredible aspirations for my work, ministry, leadership and for changing the world; and I even had a plan and incremental goals to reach those objectives. Yet, I had no real strategy for life balance or family success.

I set an early pace and an unhealthy lifestyle, which Mary resisted gra-ciously for 15 years until she'd had enough. She had been forced to live as an emotionally single mom raising a family without a father. I was emotion-ally absent, pursuing dreams outside my family's season, which set the course of our family life into a spinning mode.

When life starts to spin, it begins small and slow and gains power and mo-mentum over time, just like a tornado. "Life spin," as we define it, is when your life feels like it's moving too fast and you can't seem to catch your breath or find time for healthy rest and relaxation. It's all-consuming. We use the acronym SPIN to represent these elements: *Seasons, Priorities, Isolation, Neglect*—all of which must be in balance to enable a person to make healthy life choices.

How you deal with SPIN predicts how well you will move from hectic to healthy. But it's more than that; it's about relationships, friends, soul care and forgiveness. They are all interrelated. Mary and I have experienced that when life starts to spin out of control it's not simply about getting control of your calendar or finding time for rest. These are healthy choices, but they are only a small part of what you need to do in order to move from hectic to healthy. Let's take a closer look at the SPIN acronym.

Seasons

"Season" is whatever life stage you are in. Are you married? Single? Married with kids? Single with kids? Your lifestyle should reflect your family's sea-son—a concept we refer to as Seasonality. When you live life out of its cor-rect season, life begins to SPIN.

Priorities

Where do you spend your time and money? Where is your heart? A person's priorities are often reflected in his or her calendar and finances. The key to setting healthy priorities is not found in aligning them but in balancing them by giving the appropriate amount of time to the more significant peo-ple in your life—namely, your family.

Isolation

Do you feel isolated, or alone? Taking time to be alone to refresh and refill is very productive and healthy. But withdrawing from others in an effort to hide increases life SPIN because it removes accountability to others.

Neglect

Neglect isn't always an obvious choice. Most people would not willfully neglect their family. However, neglect can be a byproduct of doing too much in another area of life that, by default, brings neglect to those who are most important to you. When this happens, life can pick up speed and quickly become unbalanced.

When you live life out of its *Season,* and spend most of your time on wrong *Priorities,* you begin to live an *Isolated* life and drift into the *Neglect* of your soul care and your relationships. This combination of SPIN creates a perfect storm that can leave a significant damage path as it moves through your life. Nothing good can come from it. The faster you SPIN, the more you are in danger of hurting others and your own soul.

Without a doubt, SPIN will eventually lead to sin. With that in mind, Mary and I want to talk about *more* than SPIN and recovering from it. We want to talk about what's next—you know, life *after* the effects of SPIN. But first you need to know the process that got us there.

A Short Attention Span

It wasn't too long ago that I was sitting in a staff meeting at church discussing a book on balance that we had decided to study as a team. To be honest, I was answering the questions around the circle that day pretty well. I would give myself an 8 or a 9 on a scale of 1 to 10. My answers were quick, biblical and subtle enough to not cause any heads to turn. You could hear an occasional "Hmmm" and "Yes, Lord" coming from me, and others in the room, to add that spiritual kick to the study, but that was about it.

The irony was that this six-week study on balance took us 12 weeks to finish because we were all too busy! When the 12 weeks were up, so was the margin. We all went right back to doing more with less, stoking our workaholic tendencies—excuse me, workaholic *traits*—and our emotional and spiritual unhealthiness. For me, gaining some form of life balance was something I did in a short study or maybe for a season or summer at most.

Fast-forward a few years. Mary and I were having a pretty strong disagreement about my time commitments away from home. I told her that she married a pastor, and like any other pastor, I didn't have a 9-to-5 job and never would. I said she would have to continue to get used to my schedule. After all, there were people who needed Jesus; and we had programs to run, volunteers to lead and problems to solve.

When you are "working for Jesus," things like soul care, relationship management, spiritual health, balance and margin are right at the tip of your tongue but often far from your heart. At least they were far from mine. I talked about them and even had good intentions about making them happen. I have 11 devotional books on my shelf to prove my intentions, and I can talk "spiritual" with the best of them. But the bottom line is that deterioration happens over time. The word itself implies falling from a higher to a lower level in quality. So, I guess you could say that my ministry was healthy, but I was not. My spiritual and emotional life was deteriorating—going from a higher quality to a lower one, and it was impacting the people I loved the most.

I needed renewal. When people talk about spiritual renewal, they often think "get right with Jesus." That's what I thought. However (and I may step on some theological toes here), it's more than that. Yes, it's about being spiritually and emotionally healthy, but it's also about having your priorities in the right order and being accountable for those priorities to someone who truly cares about you. So how do you go about spiritual renewal, or getting back to a relationship with Jesus that's alive and vibrant again? You allow Him to control your choices and permeate all areas of your life.

How God Got My Attention

I believe that a person changes because he or she hurts enough to be motivated to change, or learns enough to want to change. The latter was not true for me. I "knew" how to change; I had even preached and taught on the subject. I knew so much about how to "act" that I didn't have to change—I could fake it.

For me, change usually comes through pain: the death of one of our children; my wife in the hospital for 52 days in a row; a severe injury to one of our sons, whom the doctor said would be blind. God seems to get my attention through hurt and pain. I had to run my wife, my kids, my friends and myself to the edge of destruction before God got my attention.

During the last year of serving in ministry at a church, there were a number of times when I would just break down and cry in my car for no apparent reason. I couldn't put my finger on anything specific. I started to withdraw from friends and what was left of an emotional connection with my family. The clinical term is depression. I was depressed. No hobbies, no outlet, no margin, no balance, no laughing, no close friends, no kidding. To put it mildly, my life was ready to go *splat*.

When I left my position at church, I had accrued just under 300 hours of vacation time—that's a little more than seven weeks. It's what I call "accumulated sickness," and it warranted a trip to a counselor to help me get a healthy perspective on life.

Mary had been trying to get us in to see a counselor for years—asking kindly and gently; prodding, praying and then conceding that it wouldn't happen because of my rationalization that people in ministry didn't go to counselors; it would acknowledge that we *didn't* have it all together.

Well, I eventually hurt enough that I had to change. My addiction to ministry (yes, you can be addicted to ministry) was like any other addiction: it was unhealthy. The definition of addiction is "the state of being enslaved to a habit or practice or to something that is psychologically or physically habit-forming to such an extent that its cessation causes severe trauma."[1] This addiction, manifested in my desire to *do* the best and *be* the best, put me in a situation that, over time, was less than healthy. I became bitter, angry and unforgiving. In fact, I was downright toxic.

Lack of time alone with God and with my wife and family were unhealthy trends that invaded and then defined my life. These trends threatened my marriage and permeated my very being. I was dangerously close to crossing lines outside of my marriage that could not be erased. Something radical had to be done. Something had to change. I was tired, on edge, finished . . . but not done.

I had to face the reality that my wife had become a single working mom who was trying to run our company and nonprofit ministry and raise three kids. I was a dad who was there in the morning and back in the evening, and that's about it. I didn't help around the house or help the kids with schoolwork. I was constantly argumentative and generally on edge. I didn't want to go home because there was always something to be done at church or in one of our outside ministries. I didn't want to open email, because I didn't want to engage another problem or deal with someone who disagreed with me or had a "word" from the Lord for me. However, when I was faced with losing the ones who were most precious to me, I had to change.

Fast-forward five years. I am finally on the road to emotional and spiritual health. At least I'm far enough down that road to know what health looks like. Let me tell you this: it isn't easy. But I can at least take a vacation and not feel guilty. And I would rather be with my family or do things with my family than be anywhere or do anything else. Not only do I say that, but I have also started to practice it. I don't say it from a position of arrogance but from lessons learned through pain.

We spent 18 months in counseling. We still have a lot to learn about being emotionally and spiritually healthy, but we are progressing. We, especially me (Craig), have a lot to learn about priorities and how to really live them out without guilt or pretending that we have it all together.

So how do you find renewal? How do you find balance? How do you find health? I guess I could say something like "have a daily quiet time" or "pray more authentically" or "read a book on balance," but honestly, aren't we past that by now? How about letting the pure power of Jesus Christ take control of you? How about actually living the priorities you talk about—God-family-ministry? No formula, just one broken person talking to another, saying, "I love you, and we are going to do this journey together, no matter what."

If there is one thing I have learned, it's this: We are *all* messed up. I think that's why Jesus came—to give His life for ours. Yes, He came to pave a way to heaven, but He also came to provide us with hope in this world, not just hope in the next. So how do you get spiritually renewed? It's not simply from a book, sermon or lecture; but it could be a combination of learning enough that you want to get renewed, or hurting enough that you have to get renewed. Either way will work.

It could also come from an unknown direction. Perhaps from someone's story of being broken and then rebuilt—someone who had to come to grips with the reality around him and make a change.

Jacob Chose Seasonal Living

The idea of living your life according to its season—the principle of *seasonality*—is a biblical one when it comes to crops, planting, harvesting and even people. When you understand SPIN and what causes it, you will be in a position to not only STOP, but also to construct a healthy PACE and continue to WALK through each season. We will talk about seasonal priorities in chapter 10, but it's important to provide a foundation at this point for what it means for you to live in YOUR season. To do that, we would like you to take a look at Jacob and Esau. You know their big story, right? About deception, a pot of stew and a birthright? The story we want to highlight is, in many ways, a small continuation of their epic birthright drama, and it's an important one.

But first let's revisit the well-known story: Jacob and his mom, Rebekah, cheated Esau—his brother, her son—out of his birthright by conspiring to deceive Jacob's dad and her husband, Isaac (yes, there were even dysfunctional families back then) to give Jacob, Rebekah's favorite son, the birthright that should have gone to Esau as eldest. Well, you know the story. Mom cooks some stew, Jacob throws on some of Esau's clothes and adds a little hair from the goat skin to the back of his hands and neck. The stew and the disguise combined with Isaac's exceptionally poor eyesight created a diabolical plan of deception that was successfully executed.

We remind you of these highlights of the story so that we can emphasize Esau's response. Clearly, you don't need a *Birthright for Dummies* book to see that Esau is going to lose it big-time when he finds out that his dad, Isaac, blessed the wrong son, not to mention that his brother and mom were in on it.

This entire saga plays out in the book of Genesis, chapter 27, but take special note of Esau's last recorded words about his brother: "I will kill my brother Jacob" (Gen. 27:41, *NIV*). Those are not endearing words. We bring this up because the next time it is recorded that Esau and Jacob see each other is an amazing story of fear, assumption, intrigue, tension and surprise (see Gen. 33). It would make a great movie.

After Jacob received the firstborn birthright blessing from his father, Isaac, he left Beersheba and traveled north to Uncle Laban's house. While living with Laban, Jacob married Leah and then her sister, Rachel. It is recorded that during that time Jacob had 12 children—11 boys and 1 girl. Brother Esau left Beersheba as well and traveled south to see his Uncle Ishmael, and he married one of Ishmael's daughters.

Now Jacob is on the move with his entire family, his herds, groceries, house (tents). This is no easy task. He is also traveling south . . . toward Esau. Genesis 32 gives us some insight about how Jacob was feeling as he started this road trip.

Jacob sent messengers to his brother Esau, in Edom, the land of Seir. He told them, "Give this message to my master Esau: 'Humble greetings from your servant Jacob! I have been living with Uncle Laban until recently, and now I own oxen, donkeys, sheep, goats, and many servants, both men and women. I have sent these messengers to inform you of my coming, hoping that you will be friendly to us'" (Gen. 32:3–5).

Did you see the last part of that message? Jacob is "hoping that you [Esau] will be friendly to us." Apparently, Esau's last recorded words—"I will kill my brother, Jacob"—were still on Jacob's mind.

The messengers returned with some intimidating news. They told Jacob that Esau was on his way to meet him and he was bringing an army of 400 men! Genesis 32:7 tells us Jacob's response: "Jacob was terrified at the news." Verse 11 records his prayer: "O LORD, please rescue me from my brother, Esau. I am afraid that he is coming to kill me, along with my wives and children." Jacob sent one more gift to Esau to try to ease the impending blow, but Esau kept coming. Genesis 33 records Jacob and Esau's reunion, and it didn't go as Jacob had thought . . . it went much better.

Once Jacob saw Esau coming, he went out to meet him and bowed before him, expecting the worst. But Esau grabbed Jacob and gave him a hug! *What?!* They were both in tears. Jacob's tears were tears of "Praise God! I'm not dead." We can only assume that Esau's tears were tears of joy in seeing his brother again, although it's not recorded.

Once the greetings were out of the way, Jacob introduced Esau to his family. After the official greetings, Esau says, "Well, let's be going. . . . I will stay with you and lead the way" (Gen. 33:12). Isn't that a typical first-born, driven personality statement? I don't think he was being rude. I think that was just how he was wired—natural leader with a take-control personality. Either way, it was time to go, according to Esau.

Let's pause here for a moment. We gave you the background to this story to highlight Jacob's response to Esau's statement, "Let's be going. . . . I will stay with you and lead the way." Notice that it wasn't a question. Like most leaders, Esau didn't ask; he told. He cast a vision and expected Jacob to follow. The natural default of a leader is to lead. They vision cast. They move. Your boss doesn't ask your permission to do something. Your boss doesn't ask when you are taking a vacation and then plan changes around your schedule. The boss makes the plans and sets the pace and moves; and you need to gauge your speed accordingly.

Do you see what is happening here in Genesis 33? Before Esau arrived, Jacob was afraid. He was back in the presence of his brother who he cheated out of his birthright. He was afraid when he heard that Esau was coming with 400 of his friends. He had offered gifts, twice, to possibly ease the potential confrontation, but to no avail. Then Esau says, "Move out; let's go!"

Now Jacob has a choice. For me, it would have been easy. I would have said, "Gals, kids, pack it up; we are out of here." I would have felt lucky to still be alive and most likely would have simply gone with him. Jacob didn't do that. He said no! He said no politely, but he still said no. His answer to Esau is found in Genesis 33:13-14: "But Jacob said to him, 'My lord knows that the children are tender and that I must care for the ewes and cows that are nursing their young. If they are driven hard just one day, all the animals will die. So let my lord go on ahead of his servant, while I move along slowly at the pace of the droves before me and that of the children, until I come to my lord in Seir'" (*NIV*).

Jacob's response is something I (Craig) wish I could have mustered within myself when making decisions about life balance and priorities. Jacob's response is something we should all take to heart and dig a little deeper to see how or if, in some small way, it applies to us.

The point is that we are all in different seasons of life—single, married, married with young kids, married with older kids, married with kids in college. The goal is to make decisions for you and your family in the context of *your* season. We can't tell you what choices to make. We simply ask that you consider the best possible decisions that will set the pace of your life for each season.

So what did Jacob say that can make so much difference in our lives? It was the statement, "Go on ahead while I move along slowly at the pace of the droves before me and that of the children." Jacob's *season* of life was married with kids. His season dictated his time commitments, priorities and decisions. And he made this decision and told Esau about it when not too long before he was scared to death that Esau was going to kill him! The last answer I would give someone I thought wanted to kill me is no. But Jacob knew that traveling at a PACE that Esau (translated boss or leader or pastor or CEO) could and would travel would not be healthy for *his family*. Would the answer have been different if Jacob was single? Maybe, but we'll never know. What we do know is that his decision matched his life's season, and it was a healthy choice.

How do we handle season-of-life decisions? I know how I handled them in the past. I simply made the choices that fed a workaholic, dream-setting, goal-achieving only child who wanted to change the world. I inadvertently jeopardized my relationship with my wife and children because I expected them to maintain *my* PACE, not *theirs*. It was an unfortunate decision on my part, but redeemable because we have a God who not only reveals truth but who also redeems it.

What season are you in? SPIN begins when you live your life out of its seasonal balance. The four chapters that make up this section on SPIN describe how fast and out of balance life can become. Living your life out of its *Seasonal* balance is just the beginning. When you add mismanaged *Priorities*, *Isolation* from others and the *Neglect* of your own soul care, you have a perfect storm that moves SPIN from a top to a tornado that uproots anything in its path.

Perhaps it's time for all of us to rise up and say a collective no to *doing* and a collective yes to *being*. I hope you will continue on the journey you have started with this book's content as we unpack life balance together.

Mary and I don't want this to be just another book or study. We hope it will be a transformational process for you of life lived in balance. Are you in? Good. Because what you read next will sound like the beginning of the end for our family. It was actually the beginning of the rest of our lives together.

I've already told you the words I read in Mary's journal. But now we want you to know the details and understand what led her to such desperation.

Journals Don't Lie

It was a Sunday evening not unlike any other. I (Craig) went to work early, came home late, ate dinner by myself, got into a brief discussion with my wife—okay, an argument—then went upstairs to turn on Sports Center. I became disinterested with the show during a commercial and started cleaning up the room a bit. I looked under the couch, since this was a favorite place for our boys, Cameron and Alec, to hide Legos, action figures and candy wrappers. What I found was a journal.

I reached for the book and opened it. It was Mary's journal. One night while crying out to God, she noted her thoughts about a God who was deeply connected to her and a husband who was not; a God who would not let her down and a husband who had; a God who would never fail her and a husband who did. I wish I could say I responded with compassion, grace and empathy, and a true desire to change. Unfortunately, I was not healthy enough emotionally or spiritually to respond that way. Instead, reading the journal made me feel irritated, upset, mad, hurt. And to be honest, a little scared.

The words "I have decided to take the kids and leave" and "I hate my husband" were the ones that hurt the most. I slammed the journal shut and walked downstairs, my heart beating faster with every step. Once I got to the bottom, I was ready for an argument. What happened next was both painful and life changing. Mary tells it in her own words.

I (Mary) pulled into the garage and started unloading the groceries, my mind already on the next tasks ahead: make dinner, get the kids ready for bed, put a load of clothes in the wash. I looked up to see Craig standing in the garage, holding my journal. *Oh no!* I thought. *I sure hope he didn't read that. He wouldn't do that, would he? That's private stuff. And besides, I had shoved it way under the couch upstairs where he would NEVER find it.* The look on his face told me otherwise.

"I *hate* my husband." He quoted the words I had written in my journal just a few weeks earlier. I knew we were in for another heated argument, and this one was in uncharted waters.

Just three days before this, I had summoned the courage to tell Craig that I had made an appointment with a Christian counselor for the following Tuesday. I told him I had called a friend who was a counselor and asked for a referral to someone who would be a good fit for Craig. She recommended us to Jim, who counseled pastors and also had experience as a senior pastor. I was thrilled to find out that Jim didn't attend our church but had an office not far from our home. It seemed like a perfect fit. I was scared to make the call, but I was desperate. If this didn't work, and I couldn't get Craig to go to see Jim, then *I* was going to need help; so either way, I had decided that I was going to counseling with or without Craig.

After 15 years of marriage and too many arguments to count, I was done. Finished. I was ready to leave Craig. In my mind, it would be easier to be a single mom and raise the kids alone. At least I wouldn't have to deal with his personal issues and ministry issues anymore. I have my bachelor's degree and master's degree in speech therapy, and a teaching credential as well. I was confident that I could get a job in my chosen field. I had already been out looking for a home to rent in a neighborhood that was close to the kids' school. I just needed the courage to go through with it.

Of course, when I told Craig about the counseling appointment, he was upset. He told me that he wasn't going to see the counselor, and I told him that I was going without him. My words to him were, "I'm tired of living a lie." He replied, "What are you talking about? I have no idea what you mean by that."

Now, the journal changed all that. What I had planned to tell him in the security of a counselor's office he had read in the pages of my journal. He knew that I had written the words "I hate my husband"; he knew that I hated the life we were living, day in and day out. I was so disconnected from him that I truly thought I hated him at that point. The reality was that I hated our life together, if you could call it "together."

I felt like we were living a lie inside our fishbowl life. Everyone thought we were this cute couple with a great marriage and great kids—the perfect family. Craig's high-profile job in ministry meant that he was often asked to speak not only at our church but also for other churches and conferences all over the United States. Both of us had written curriculum for children's ministry that hundreds of churches were using in their small groups, not to mention our own church; and people looked up to us. Not only that, but we were small-group leaders of a marriage group, and couples came to our house weekly.

I had to come to grips with the fact that people were going to find out the truth about us—that we didn't have it all together; that our marriage wasn't great; that we fought. That being married to "fun" Craig was not all that fun. In fact, it wasn't fun at all. It was just a bunch of work, and it was lonely. I felt like a baby-sitter, a cook and a maid in my own home. I was a ministry widow at best.

The truth is, Craig and I were business partners who slept in the same bed but never really connected. I felt unloved, unknown and unappreciated. I knew there was a giant wall between the two of us, and no matter how many books on marriage I read, how much I prayed or how much I tried to be the "perfect wife," I couldn't fix our marriage. And I was tired of trying. For me, this *season* was about to come to an abrupt end.

2

PRIORITIES

There is only one person that came to change the world.
And you just work for Him.

JIM MASTELLAR

Me, Myself and I

It's tough to come to the end of something without knowing that it began. How on earth did Mary get to the place of *I hate my husband* without my knowing? Why didn't she tell me? Why didn't she try to get my attention? Well, apparently she had been trying for a very long time; I just didn't want to hear it. I was busy trying to change the world, while my relationship with my wife and kids was going down the drain. I wish I could tell you that at this point in our story it got better. It didn't. It got worse, much worse.

I (Mary) am not quite sure how Craig didn't see the issues we were facing. Our problems hadn't suddenly come up in the last year or so. They started the first week we came back from our honeymoon. I can vividly remember that Saturday night. I was making dinner, and Craig came in and kissed me on the cheek and said, "I'll be back later. I have to go to church."

"What?" I replied. "Church right now? Why? Aren't we going to eat dinner together and hang out tonight? I thought maybe we could watch a movie and—"

Craig interrupted and said, "You *know* I go to church every Saturday night to prepare for Sunday morning. I have to go to church and get ready. I'll be home later." He did come home later, much later. When he got home, his dinner had been sitting on the counter for five hours. I was mad, and I was hurt. How could he leave his new wife home alone on a Saturday night? Didn't he love me? Didn't he want to be with me?

My thoughts went back to our dating experience. I never wanted to marry a pastor. I had actually broken up with Craig at one point when I realized where he was going with his life. I didn't want to be on that train, if you know what I mean. But later, I felt the call to ministry separately from Craig, and I decided it was worth the risk, but not without a conversation. I can clearly remember having a conversation with him before we got married about ministry and time commitment with family. I grew up in a ministry family and was well aware of the time commitment given to others and the ministry outside of the home. I had asked Craig to promise me it wouldn't be like that in our family. He *had* promised; he made the commitment to prioritize family over ministry, but it never happened.

I felt a separation in our relationship almost immediately. I had a choice to make: I could either jump in and do ministry with him or not see him at all. So I jumped in. I started volunteering at every event he was doing. I was a small-group leader on Monday nights, director on Wednesday nights, youth leader Friday nights, a teacher on Sunday mornings; and that was just during the school year. The summer schedule was another level of busyness in ministry. We did a sixth grade missions trip for 10 days, a week of Summer Spectacular, a week of summer camp; and on the other weeks of summer, we ran Monday Madness, Wild Wednesdays and Fireproof Fridays. The only week we could take a vacation, according to Craig, was the week that the Music Ministry hosted a Music Camp for kids.

Each year during our anniversary week, the week of July 26, was the traditional time we inherited to do our Summer Spectacular, and Craig did not change it. For years we spent our anniversary at Summer Spectacular. For me this was another example of how ministry came before our marriage.

If that wasn't enough, Craig was asked to serve at another church, and after prayerful consideration, we started a new journey. This changed things dramatically for us, but not for the better. Craig's days started at 7:00 AM, not necessarily because he had to but because he wanted to. He was never home before 7:00 PM in the evening. It was at that time that he decided he needed to write a book. One night after coming home from a meeting, he told me that everyone there had written a book. So his evening hours were spent on the computer. He also began writing a discipleship curriculum for the kids at church and speaking at events and conferences around the country.

Priorities were unhealthy and the momentum of life spinning us started to pick up speed. I saw us pulling further and further away from each other, but I had no idea what to do about it other than talk with him. We would start a conversation that would end in an argument, and things would get better for a while. Craig would get home at a more reasonable hour, plan a date or two with me or we would take a vacation; but it never lasted long. Soon things were right back to "work, work, work," all day and all night.

As the years passed, we had children, which intensified the need for Craig to be home more often. I needed my husband, and the kids needed their daddy. There were many more conversations about priorities and not being home enough, but it really did no lasting good. Craig would tell me that I was going to have to get used to it, because he would never have a nine-to-five schedule. I was a ministry widow with three young children. I grew frustrated at the realization that there may not be a way out of our situation. I felt trapped and completely alone.

As I (Craig) look back at Mary's journal and her repeated attempts to get my attention, I now know how she arrived at the words *I hate my husband*. If someone other than Mary had described the guy you just read about, I would say, "That guy is an idiot. Why isn't he spending time with his wife and children? Why is he out running around trying to save the world? He should have more balance than that." However, I couldn't see that it was me.

There is a similar story in Scripture when a guy didn't get it. You may recall the story of the prophet Nathan and his conversation with King David recorded in 2 Samuel 12:1-7:

> So the LORD sent Nathan the prophet to tell David this story: "There were two men in a certain town. One was rich, and one was poor. The rich man owned many sheep and cattle. The poor man owned nothing but a little lamb he had worked hard to buy. He raised that little lamb, and it grew up with his children. It ate from the man's own plate and drank from his cup. He cuddled it in his arms like a baby daughter. One day a guest arrived at the home of the rich man. But instead of killing a lamb from his own flocks for food, he took the poor man's lamb and killed it and served it to his guest."
>
> David was furious. "As surely as the LORD lives," he vowed, "any man who would do such a thing deserves to die! He must repay four lambs to the poor man for the one he stole and for having no pity."
>
> Then Nathan said to David, "You are that man!'"

Nathan weaves this emotional story, waits for David's response, and then delivers the devastating truth-filled pronouncement, "You are that man!" How typical is this scenario? I know it's true of my life. I can see everyone else's sin but can't seem to get a proper reading on the guy in the mirror. We seem to see others with 20/20 vision, but things are a little fuzzy when we read our own chart.

How on earth could I be a good leader in ministry but a terrible leader at home? The answer is an easy one: I *wanted* to be a good leader at church and, as a result, that's where I put my time, effort, energy and life. The books I read were about leadership, vision, building and advancing. The books and articles I wrote were about the same things. Mary would try to get me to read a book with her on marriage or relationships, but I wasn't interested in that. I would start reading to appease her but would never finish.

Why I wanted to be a good leader at church is another question entirely and would fill another book. We will take a look at this motivation in chapter 5, because it does contribute to what drives us. Simply put, the reason for my apparent dysfunction was how I set my *priorities*. I had two sets of them. The first set is what I now call my *verbal priorities*. You know, the ones you claim to have. They usually go something like this if you were asked: "Hey, Craig, what would you say are your top three priorities in life right now?" "Hey, thanks for asking. [Spiritual smile] I would have to say, God, Family, then Church." Can I get a testimony? Anyone?

The second set of priorities is what I call my *actionable priorities*. These are the priorities I actually lived out. God didn't make the top three after a while, and neither did my family. A look at my calendar told the whole story. My priorities were me, myself and I. The speaking engagements, leadership meetings, summits and services were things I loved to do, wanted to do and eventually had to do. No, I didn't *have* to do them—no one was holding me by the throat and demanding that I do them. It was more of an addiction. Just like the next drink or drug, I felt compelled to, motivated to, *had to* get the next fix, the next adrenaline rush, the next ministry high. Why have 500 people at a summer event when you could have 5,000?

I know the biblical answer is because everyone needs Jesus. But how about my wife? What about those three kids at home? Don't they need Jesus too? I wish I had known that different seasons of life call for different priorities. This begs the questions, "What is your season?" "What are your priorities?" The best way to answer the first question is to look at a family photo, then look at your calendar. Does your time appropriately reflect that picture? Mine did not. Raising a family; spending time with them; connecting with my spouse; being a role model for my children; being present for dinner, sports, school activities, a walk or riding a bike—all these things take time. My time was focused in a different direction.

I can remember one of the key moments in my life a few years ago when my son Alec was playing with a bug in the yard. After some back-and-forth chitchat, Mary asked him, "Alec, what do you want to be when you grow up?" Alec said, "An entomologist." I honestly didn't know that *he* knew what that word meant. I was about to ask him, but before I could, he added, "I wanted to be a pastor, but it takes too much time away from your family."

I wasn't ready for that, nor did I have time to prepare a comeback. I was stunned, stopped in my tracks, spinning, reeling from his comment. A flood of emotions, from upset to angry to sad, flooded my body. I had no words. Alec wasn't arguing; he wasn't being confrontational; he was simply answering the question Mary asked him. How did he come to that decision? What was his thought process? Did he outline it, write a paper, do the appropriate research, or poll a sample group? No, he just made a truthful statement in the way that only a nine-year-old can. His statement reflected how he felt—that Dad was not around as much as he would like and, as a result, he didn't want to be in *that* line of work. Family was more important to him.

A comment like that can linger with you; it did with me. I don't prefer guilt as a motivator. It tends to be depressing, and the emotional byproduct feels unhealthy to me. Our enemy wants that guilt to swirl around, stagnate, fester and turn into disease. It's more productive for him in the long run. The words I kept mulling over in my mind were, *You are blowing it. You are a terrible dad. Look at the time you lost. You can't get a do-over for the last nine years. You are more concerned about the families in your church than you are with your own family. You spend 10 hours a day trying to make the world a better place while neglecting your wife and children in the process.*

If you picked up this book looking for answers to your own overwork, then great, you are already *in*. If someone handed this book to you and asked you to read it, you are about 14 chapters away from an intervention. Either way, let us offer you some encouragement and comfort from God's Word and our own experience.

Dead Man Walking

First the life experience. Yes, I was blowing it with my priorities. My family picture did not reflect my calendar. I felt guilt, but I wasn't motivated by it; life just felt heavy. In fact, the guilt contributed to my life SPIN. However, the past four years have taught me something about the power of the Holy Spirit and redemption. God is a master at bringing life from death.

Remember Lazarus? When Jesus heard that Lazarus was seriously ill, He decided to stay where He was for another two days before traveling to Judea to see him. Jesus said, "Lazarus's sickness will not end in death. No, it is for the glory of God. I, the Son of God, will receive glory from this" (John 11:4). Now, let me reveal my sinful, sarcastic self here. I'm sure you have never felt this way, nor would you have felt this way in this situation; but travel with me for a moment back in time to this very moment. If I were to put myself in Mary's (not my Mary) or Martha's shoes, I may have responded this way to this situation.

"Okay, Jesus, thanks for that. Lazarus's sickness won't end in death [see verse 4]? News flash, he *did* die. To make matters worse, You *let* him die. You delayed; You stayed in that other city for two additional days [see verse 6] before coming here. And to top it all off, You say You're *glad* You weren't here [see verse 15], and You go so far as to say that it was for *my sake* You weren't here? Seriously? I don't get it."

Have you ever noticed how Jesus seems to view things differently from the way we do? When the messengers came to Him that day to deliver the news about Lazarus's sickness, He was recorded as saying, "Lazarus's sickness will not end in death" (John 11:4). Notice the wording. Jesus didn't say he wouldn't die; He said that it will not *end* in death. And it didn't. I have a tendency to view death as the end, the final step. If something dies, it's dead. Jesus doesn't see it that way. He seems to think death is part of a process.

Sometimes we think Jesus is distant and detached when He is simply delaying. Why does He do that? Perhaps to deepen our faith, bring more glory to Himself and to allow the *process* of dying to play out. It appears to me that healing someone who is sick pales in comparison to raising someone from the dead. Yet, isn't that why He came? "I came that they may have life, and have it abundantly" (John 10:10, *NASB*).

What we are saying is that no matter how long you have felt disconnected from your spouse, your children, your family, it's not over. It's not dead, and that should be encouraging to you. God brings life from death; He allows second chances and time to change. It's not easy. No, it's not. Death takes an emotional toll. It's painful. It *feels* like the end. It feels like there is no tomorrow, but there is. Resurrection and redemption are Jesus' creed. As hard as it is to conceive in our finite minds, death is simply a process to Him. So when you feel like you've blown it with your priorities, and death is looming, you can rejoice because a new day is just around the corner.

Jesus provided the power to raise Lazarus, but Lazarus still had to walk. Tiny step by tiny step, bandaged, bruised and bewildered, he had to walk out of a tomb that had the smell of death. I'm sure it wasn't easy for him to shuffle out the way he did. We can relate a bit to Lazarus. Mary and I had to take some active steps to move from a hectic path to a path of health. We rearranged priorities and set some new ones, and one step at a time, bandaged, bruised and bewildered, we had to walk out. There were days, months, when I felt like these were impossible steps to take. Occasionally, I lost my emotional and spiritual balance and ended up facedown until someone helped me back up and removed my bandages. Please hear us when we say that God brings life from death, resurrection from ruin, but you must put in some work. Jesus brought Lazarus back from death, but Lazarus had to respond and walk out one step at a time. And so will you.

Healthy Thoughts or Maybe Nots

My parents (Craig) taught me at a very young age to have an incredibly strong work ethic and do all things with excellence. I still believe in those things today. Leading with passion, having a strong work ethic and a desire to change the world are good things. It's when they are mixed together in a stubborn mind like mine that they can begin to warp. Among other things, they warped because of my inability to keep my priorities in check and in balance.

When someone has an incredibly strong work ethic, a gift of leadership and a passion to change the world, there can be a powerful effect when combined that can produce results yet leave those closest to you in a wake of disaster. As a leader, I enjoy casting vision and inspiring people to be the best they can be. I love to rally people toward a common objective. I love to encourage, equip, energize and empower others to lead, to push on and to realize their potential. I would often use sayings that communicated a desire and passion to motivate and inspire. "I will change the world!" and "Whatever it takes!" were part of my vocabulary and philosophy, yet I never stopped to really think about them. The statements appear to be inspirational and motivational—the stuff that brings to mind movies like *Chariots of Fire*, *Rocky* and *Remember the Titans*. They certainly wouldn't be viewed as negative or wrong.

"I will change the world!" What do you think? Healthy thought, or maybe not? When Mary and I had a standing 2:15 PM Tuesday appointment with our counselor, Jim, I affectionately called this time "my 2:15 butt kicking." During one appointment, when we were just about finished, I said, "Jim, I have a question. Aren't we supposed to change the world?" His response caught me a little off guard. He laughed as he sat back in his chair. His reaction was disarming and resonant to me; it put me at ease. It actually lured me into a momentary state of self-confidence regarding the topic. It was as if he meant to say, "Of course, Craig, we are all out to change the world." Well, it turns out, I read the room wrong. He paused for a while, and with a smile still on his face, he leaned forward and spoke directly into my soul. He said, "Craig, there is only one person that came to change the world. And *you* just work for Him." That statement entered my ears and went to my head and exploded in my heart. Jim's comment hit me hard like a wave crashes on the beach. It was cold and harsh as it pinned me to the gritty, sandy bottom; yet in some weird way, it had a calming and releasing effect that I cannot completely explain.

That was a defining moment for me. It helped bring about change. I could almost feel the pressure of such a lofty goal subside as the wave that quickly hit and held me under began to retreat. I could feel the adrenaline release from my body as a sudden calmness moved into my life. The Holy Spirit mixed with Jim's words stuck in my soul. It made sense to me. I don't need to change the world. I just work for the Guy who does.

"Whatever it takes!" What do you think? Healthy thought, or maybe not? Whatever else it takes to get the job done was the last line in a couple of job descriptions I have seen over the years. It was the last line in the job descriptions I wrote for my staff. I love this statement! It resonates with me. It speaks of commitment, sacrifice, surrender and survival—all to make a difference. It prompts me to action, makes me want to charge the hill to win through perseverance and tenacity. It serves as a sports slogan and is painted on the walls of countless training rooms in schools and universities all over the world. It says, "Don't give up, don't give in, don't give out!" and, to be honest, it fits nicely with my firstborn/only child order and type A, driven-leader personality. However, "whatever it takes" suggests that there is a cost involved, and depending on what you are doing and the season you are doing it in, there can be a *substantial* cost.

Perhaps "whatever it takes" changes to "what it took," and the "take" was your life, your health, your emotions, your family and your friends. Think of "whatever it takes" as a target, not the arrow. Understanding SPIN and learning STOP requires sacrifice and surrender. It requires commitment to not give up, give in or give out. Where I got into trouble with this phrase and moved it from a healthy thought to a "maybe not" was in the context in which I applied it. I applied this phrase to my work style, church ministries and outside ministries, but not my family. When a new opportunity would come along, I would take it without hesitation. Hey, whatever it takes, right?

I would be asked to speak at a church or conference, which presented an opportunity to advance the Kingdom, and without hesitation I would take it. Whatever it takes, right? I would have a new idea that I felt compelled to act on. It fueled my entrepreneurial spirit and helped people advance to where God wanted them to be, so without hesitation, I would do it. Whatever it takes, right? Each time I echoed "whatever it takes," I took an unhealthy step away from my family. My "whatever it takes" attitude started out with pure intentions and passionate resolve to know Christ and make Him known. It's the passion of "whatever it takes" that jumps out to you in the battle cry to make a difference in this world. It appeals to all of us. Teach one more, reach one more, preach one more.

The difficulty was that over time my "whatever it takes" attitude evolved. Yes, it was my choice, but somehow I can see the enemy standing in front of the orchestra of my life with his fiery conductor's wand, setting the tempo, and I followed every beat. It's the little things that make the little differences that make the big differences. Once your life starts to spin, you must jump to the next slogan or scenario to continue to manufacture that "feel good" adrenaline rush that not only sustains you but also drives you on to more. You end up doing more than you were designed for. Then the SPIN is well underway. In my experience, the devil will always use your SPIN to tempt you to sin.

Remember, "whatever it takes" is a sacrificial statement. We are not saying that these words are wrong so much as that they may be wrong for right now. For a single person in his twenties, saying I will do "whatever it takes" to do the job or ministry could be a *healthy thought*. A single person in his twenties is in a different season than a married person. And for a married person with three children under the age of 11, saying I will do "whatever it takes" to do my job or ministry could be a *maybe not*. For "whatever it takes" to be a healthy thought in the life of a married man with children at home, he may need to rephrase the statement to read, "I will do whatever it takes to be the best husband and father I can be."

A person's well-intentioned phrases can be aimed in the wrong direction; and when that happens, they move quickly from healthy thoughts to maybe nots. You must decide how healthy thoughts play out in your life. Understanding your Season will help you to get a pretty quick read on whether or not you are living with a healthy thought or a maybe not.

3

ISOLATION

*It is doubtful that God can use a man greatly
until He has hurt him deeply.*

A. W. TOZER

Alone, or Isolated?

"You need to be an example." I'm sure you have heard those words at some point in your life. You may have even said them to your children or your spouse. Sometimes Mary and I feel like we need to be the best people, the best parents, the best spouse, the best leaders simply because people are watching. What will others think of us if we mess up or blow it? I can tell you that over time we both came to develop an onstage personality. A stage mentality suggests performance of some type. It could be a rehearsed performance or an impromptu performance; but either way, you're acting when you are on stage and not when you are off.

Mary and I have seen a number of Broadway musicals . . . some actually on Broadway. We both enjoy the drama, the music, the sets and the overall theater experience. Now, I must tell you, I am not much of an authority on the theater, like our good friends John and Debbie. They are theater people. From the sets to the songs to the storyline, they are much more than devoted enthusiasts; they are connoisseurs, expert authorities on the subject.

We have attended the theater together as couples, and their explanation and critique of the show is always intelligent and well thought out. I usually don't have much to contribute to these conversations, so I sit, smile and try not to appear stupid. However, I will tell you that it usually comes down to two things for me. First, the seats. I guess you could call me a seat snob. I would rather go to a show once and sit a few rows back from the stage than see the show twice from the back. Second, and this will hopefully explain my seat location issue, when I am close to the acting and storyline, I literally feel like I am being drawn into the production. I get involved on an emotional level with the characters. It's as if I have known them for years. I can sympathize with them and emotionally connect with their story.

Good acting *moves me*—sometimes to tears, sometimes to anger, but always with passion. Good acting connects with me in a powerful way. That's what actors are supposed to accomplish. Actors go to school for years to learn their craft. They study, rehearse and practice for hours, and for what? To emotionally *move* the people who are watching them.

Now, let me take this theater idea a step further. Acting or being on stage does not exist only in the world of theater. It can refer to theme parks as well. Let's take Disneyland as an example. It is well documented that when Disney employees enter the Magic Kingdom, they transition from employees or staff to *cast* members who are *onstage*. When they are onstage, they are working, performing, playing a role—from the ride operators to the popcorn vendors to the maintenance crews to the Disney characters. Once they start their job, they are onstage. They are in performance mode. They may not feel like acting the part, but that's their job, and they and the show must go on. They can act any way they want offstage, but they must act the right way onstage. That's what Disney cast members do; that's what theater professionals do. And I dare say, that's what some church staff members do.

That's what I did. Somehow, at some point, the concept of being *onstage* found its way into my life. When I was at church, I felt like I was onstage playing a role. I knew how to act, behave, talk, walk, smile, say amen and nod at the right time in an important meeting, as if I had rehearsed line after line in a Broadway production. I'm sorry to say that I got better with my act over time. You see, I had spent enough time in God's Word, in meetings and in front of people that I became well schooled in my new acting craft. I'd had enough quiet times, prepared enough sermons, memorized enough Scripture to fool just about anybody, fake a quiet time or stand up and preach in front of a crowd without notes.

Please understand, no one taught me how to act. No one else is to blame. I just learned how to act, and I perfected the craft over time. It was a by-product of a dying and neglected heart, and not taking my soul care seriously. I got to the point where I could speak the truth in a sermon and then violate it when I finished.

I don't want to superimpose my acting scenario on those to whom it does not apply, but it does seem like we have become so concerned about our image that we isolate ourselves as a way to protect and guide what others think of us. The stage helped me to hide in plain sight, and it also helped the transition into isolation because actors on a stage have no accountability. When you're acting, your *mask* is on.

I went from being alone to being isolated, because if I got close to people, they would see the real me. They would see inside me. I would be revealed, vulnerable, naked and ashamed. I began to feel like Adam and Eve in the garden. I was running, hiding, and God was calling out to me, "Where are you?" (Gen. 3:9, *CEV*) as if He didn't already know. I wondered, *If I show the real me, will I still have a job in church ministry?* I wouldn't hire me. Let me rephrase that, I would hire the outside me, but not the inside me. Onstage, we are politically correct and biblically savvy. We have our "act together" so to speak. Offstage is different. We aren't in costume, and we're not in character. I think everyone struggles from time to time with being open and authentic, at least we did.

I came to the conclusion that it was okay if God knew what was going on. He knows anyway, so I might as well tell Him about it. He was a safe place, a confidant. He wouldn't put me on a prayer list or in a bulletin. He wouldn't talk to my neighbor about my life or send an email to other staff members. He wouldn't let anyone know that I was in counseling. He would just listen and provide feedback through His still, small voice and His Word. *Yep, I will keep God as my confidant and friend, and I will be just fine, right?* Wrong! Yes, God wants us to talk to Him, rely on Him, worship Him, learn from Him, live for Him. But we are not to live life in isolation from other Christians. We are reminded to "not give up meeting together, as some are in the habit of doing, but let us encourage one another" (Heb. 10:25, *NIV*). God intended for us to meet, connect and do life together. We were meant to deeply share our lives with others.

When I took time to be *alone,* I would read God's Word, pray and seek Him in a deep way. I would memorize Scripture and have a general, over-all peace in my life. But when I transitioned from being alone to isolated, I neglected my soul care and became withdrawn. I spent my time recklessly and with selfish motives and ambition. When I was alone with God, I sought friends who would listen to my deepest thoughts and let me express and confess my sin without condemnation or criticism from them. Their only concern was for me and my wellbeing.

Then I went from alone to isolated. At this point, my life started spinning exponentially faster. I was living my life unconnected to its correct Season; my Priorities were not as they should be; and now I was withdrawing—Isolating myself from my wife, family and friends and moving away from any type of accountability. I wouldn't allow anyone to speak into my life. But then, why would they? On the outside—onstage—I had it all together. Inside, I was out of breath, drowning, gasping for spiritual and emotional air, but I wouldn't ask for help. Offstage—in the car, at home, in the stillness of my heart, I was exhausted, tired of the act, tired of the role. I was becoming bitter, not better. I went from a love story to a romantic comedy, from a drama to a thriller to a tragedy.

My spirit resonates with the lyrics of "Stained Glass Masquerade" by Casting Crowns when they sing, "Am I the only one who's traded in the altar for a stage . . . Only when no one is watching can we really fall apart."[1]

Counseling or Cornered?

Having effectively isolated myself from others, I was in a quandary with the idea of counseling. I tried to fake it there for a while until I realized, *I think this Jim guy can see right through me.* He could and he did.

There we sat one day in the lobby of the Marriage and Family Counseling Center. A lobby in a counseling center is a lonely place if no one else is there waiting to see someone. If by chance there is someone else in the 10-by-10 room, then it's a little better, because you can begin to play a game of "What's his/her problem?" *Look at that person—he seems bitter to me; that couple over there clearly is having some type of marital breakdown. They must really be messed up.*

I (Craig) will be perfectly honest here. My prayer while attending counseling for the first two months was, "Dear God, please don't let anyone see me!" If you are a pastor at a church and are seen with your wife at a marriage and family counselor's office, I am telling you right now, your names are going on the prayer list—"prayer list" being Greek for "gossip." That kind of news spreads faster than a forest fire squirted with gasoline.

After two months of counseling, I realized that I could not communicate, I was emotionally holding back from my wife and I was overworking. That's the short but very accurate list. I realized very soon that counseling was going to be a tough and bumpy road for me. I didn't like counseling. I felt cornered and, yes, I still didn't think I needed it. There were times when Mary and I would be heading out the door to our appointment and I would sarcastically say, "Let's go; it's time for my weekly butt kicking."

I remember one particular session when once again I was the target. While Jim, our counselor, was mid sentence, I pointed to my wife and said, "When are you going to talk to her? She has problems too, you know." That comment got me another 12 months of counseling. Clearly my issues ran deep and wide, just like the Sunday School chorus. I was pretty upset as this particular session wrapped up.

Up to that point, we would enter through the front of the counseling center and exit out the back. I didn't want anyone to know we were going to counseling or see my wife and me at a counseling center. I didn't want anyone to know we were having problems, in crisis, having difficulty in our marriage or were plain, old-fashioned messed up. Worse yet, I was a pastor with these issues. *Are you kidding me? We are supposed to have it together. We don't need counseling; we counsel others.* As this particular session ended, I was not of sound mind, and I said to myself, *To heck with it, I'm going out the front door.* I walked up front, not listening to Mary or Jim, and flung open the door loudly enough to warrant the attention of the gal sitting in the lobby. As she looked up to see us, she cracked a smile and said, "Pastor Craig, Mary, how are you?"

"Oh, we are just fine," I replied. "Thanks for asking. We just stopped by to use the restroom; why are you here?" What the heck do you say in that situation? Now the cat is out of the bag, we're on the prayer list tomorrow and life is over! To make matters much worse, Mary and I walked out to the parking lot where we proceeded to get into an argument. Yes, you are picturing it correctly. We are in the parking lot of a counseling center having an argument in front of God and the rest of the people who watched us come out of the counseling center. I was mad at Mary, our counselor, the lady in the lobby, God and anyone else I could blame.

I will never know what it meant emotionally to our Lord when Scripture tells us, "Though he was God, he did not demand and cling to his rights as God. He made himself nothing; he took the humble position of a slave and appeared in human form" (Phil. 2:6-7). He emptied Himself. The creator of the universe emptied Himself of all things God, and with humility He appeared as a man and died as a criminal for each one of us.

I don't know about you, but I like my rights. I want to be something. Yet there in the parking lot that day, I felt like I was coming to the end. Void of all pride, dignity, and whatever other word says that I felt exposed, I was completely open and vulnerable. Arguing with my wife in the parking lot of a counseling center was when I think I fully realized how messed up I was.

Thoughts that busted my onstage persona raced through my mind: *How will we survive being found out that we need help? How long will we live with the fact that we have been seen in a marriage counseling center? How long will we live with others knowing that we are messed up?* As it turns out, it's actually a long time. Now that may not sound very reassuring to you at this point, but take comfort in knowing that sometimes things have to get worse in order to get better.

The following week, we headed to our standing appointment. I actually approached this session with a different mindset. We walked in through the lobby and out through the lobby. I thought, *We're already in counseling; we've already been seen in the counseling center. What else can there be; how much worse can it get?* As we were walking out, the same woman who was there the previous week was, of course, there again. She stood up as we walked out to the lobby and gave us both a hug and then started to cry.

I didn't have the emotional bank account to handle this transaction, so I just stood there like a stiff board. She held both of us and said, "I have to tell you something. I have been trying to get my husband and kids to come to counseling for months, but they won't come. They say counseling is for weird people. Every week we drive here together, I get out and come in and they sit in the car."

Oh no! Did dad and the kids see us arguing? My mind flashed back to the previous week's parking lot meltdown and ensuing argument right there in front of God and apparently her family. She continued, "My husband and kids saw you both walk out last week." That answered the first question. Then there was an uncomfortably long pause as she adjusted herself emotionally to say what came next. She said, "They would not come in to see the counselor, but after I finished my session and got in the car they said, 'If Pastor Craig and Mary can go to counseling and not worry about what people think, then we can go to counseling.' So I just wanted to say thank you."

What just happened? God just happened. We (mostly me) were so caught up in worrying about what others thought that God had to show up. I was so worried about others viewing me, or us, as weak, troubled and messed up that I was afraid to be vulnerable. The fact is, we *are* weak, we *are* troubled, and we *are* messed up. Not just us, but you too!

Mary and I continued with our counseling for almost 18 months. It saved my life, our marriage and our future. Mary tried to get us to go to counseling for almost 10 years, to which I said either, "We don't need counseling" or "Are you kidding? What if someone sees us?" I realize now that I delayed our road to health for many years. If you are a guy reading this book, and your wife is saying to you, "Let's try counseling," then I would urge you to go. If you have more of a personality bent like mine, I would say, "Dude, shut up and listen to your wife. Go!"

Gals, this is Mary writing to you. If you feel strongly that you and your husband need help and that your marriage and family are in jeopardy, don't be afraid to take the first step. Do the research. Find a reputable Christian counselor and make an appointment. If you think your husband will respond or listen better to a man, then you may want to go to a male counselor for his benefit. It is typically easier for women to connect with a new person than it is for men. Do what you can to make it easier for your husband to go. Listen, if you leave it up to him, it may never happen; especially if he is "spinning" in his life and ministry.

I had to get to the place where I was willing to take a drastic step toward healing and help. I had to step outside of my comfort zone, admit that we had problems in our marriage and call someone. It was scary. My heart was beating so fast that I thought it would jump right out of my chest. I'll never forget that first conversation with Jim, when I was on my cell phone in the parking lot of Target and I told him that we needed marriage counseling. When he asked me if my husband would be coming with me, I had to tell him the truth: "I hope so. But if he doesn't, I will be there without him. He doesn't know I called you."

Jim gave me an appointment date and I hung up the phone and cried, both relieved and scared at the same time, and I prayed again that God would change Craig's heart and open him up to the idea of counseling. What was that coming up from inside of me . . . could it be hope? And that's one of the greatest things about a Christian counselor. They give you hope, no matter what you tell them. Because they know that with God, there is always hope. God can make something beautiful out of ugly dust. His spirit can change lives, open eyes to see things differently and mend broken hearts.

I (Craig) now know that counseling is very different from being cornered. A solid biblical counselor with the power of the Holy Spirit can move you from hectic to healthy and give you a new perspective and an actionable plan that will bring about life change and full-course correction in your life journey. God never puts you in a corner. God always has a way out that will bring glory to Him and redemptive power to you. God is not done with you yet!

We're All Messed Up

If you haven't figured it out yet, we are all messed up. Yep, that person sitting next to you at church . . . messed up. That couple in the front row . . . messed up. The people on the stage . . . messed up. Once *you* start taking off your mask, usually those around you will do the same. There will be a few reluctant ones who have a few ounces of pride left, so they will hang on to the bittersweet end, and that's okay. Smile at them, hug them, love them and give them all the grace the power of Christ has to offer.

You can explain what's involved in counseling, encourage them to go, give them articles on the topic, hand them this book, show them a YouTube video, give them the counselor's phone number and explain all the benefits of counseling, and they *still* might not go. So, you will plan an intervention—what to say, how to say it. You can't wait to say it, but before you *launch,* look in the mirror and acknowledge, "Hey, I'm really messed up," then head over to your Bible and load up on the verses that talk about grace, mercy, love and compassion. Then, with all the humbleness and gentleness of Christ, and without pointing a finger (unless you're still in front of the mirror), have the conversation. Let the Holy Spirit be the Holy Spirit, and you be you.

Today, as Mary and I speak at conferences, we hear, in city after city, that marriages and families are hurting. People seem to be caught somewhere between onstage and backstage, not understanding what the next step could be. The fear of being found out by going to counseling is terrifying. People can use that information against you, talk about you, pray about you (oops, *for* you), and generally take you down a few notches in the eyes of others. To that, I say, "Oh well." I can tell you that for us, it hasn't been easy, but I would rather live offstage with my baggage than onstage without it. It's become easier to do that.

Occasionally, Mary and I will ask people to write out one difficulty they are facing right now in their life or marriage. For those of you struggling with issues in your marriage, you are not in the minority. We don't want to paint a terrible picture of marriage or assume that everyone is struggling. We know several couples that are genuinely happy in their marriage relationship, and that's awesome! Keep going! Our conclusion, based solely on our conversations with ministerial staff and those serving in some compassion-related profession, is that they are *more likely* to struggle in their marriage than others.

Let me share a few of the responses that I've received from people around the country. I am slightly changing the words for each response, but please trust me when I tell you I am looking at the cards as they were written, by hurting individuals, and I have hundreds of them. Real life, real people, real problems. Maybe you can relate.

- "My marriage is a joke. I can't stand my husband."
- "My marriage is empty."
- "I don't feel close to my husband on any level and I am afraid to talk to him about it."
- "I love my kids more than I love my husband. Marriage is not the fairy tale I wanted it to be."

- "I'm just waiting for my kids to get to college so I can leave him. He's not around anyway. When he is home he isn't present."
- "My marriage needs help. We have very different schedules and don't communicate well, and we don't spend time together."
- "I feel so disconnected in my marriage. I feel so alone."
- "My marriage is in shambles, and I didn't care until today after listening to your story."

It may be your story; it was our story. Just like that day in counseling. God not only had a plan for us but for others as a result of our situation. The same is true for you. In other words, when you share your story, you may find yourself in a position to help others. Remember, everyone is messed up to some degree. God told the apostle Paul, who recorded those words in 2 Corinthians 12:9: " 'My gracious favor is all you need. My power works best in your weakness.' So now I am glad to boast about my weaknesses, so that the power of Christ may work through me." Your hurt could be someone else's hope. That may sound like unconventional wisdom, but God's Word is filled with this kind of thinking.

Here are two of the more familiar yet paradoxical statements in the Bible: "The last will be first, and the first will be last" (Matt. 20:16, *NIV*) and "Whoever finds his life will lose it, and whoever loses his life for my sake will find it" (Matt. 10:39, *NIV*). You can see how 2 Corinthians 12:9 fits right in here. *So, God, are You saying that when I am weak, then You are strong? When I am without strength, Your power shows up best?* I will answer for God here, from the verse of course: "YES! You got it right. My power works best in weak people."

One caveat: Do not blurt out whatever is on your mind to someone else and call that counseling, or therapy. There is a level of appropriate disclosure and authenticity that I think is necessary for your audience. Mary and I, after five years, decided to air it out here, but not *all* of it. God, Jim, family members and close friends have heard it all. The point is, someone needs to hear it all from beginning to end. Preferably someone who can help you journey through your change.

Picture the folks down the street or across the aisle at church. The ones with the two well-dressed and perfectly behaved kids, a nice car and an extremely well-kept home. The family that has it all together. The family you initially envy because you want to be like them but almost immediately despise because you can't be like them. Yeah . . . that family. They're messed up too. So you can stop withdrawing and isolating, and start choosing the path to healthy change. God will be right there with you.

4

NEGLECT

---

*And what do you benefit if you gain the whole world but lose your
own soul? Is anything worth more than your soul?*

MATTHEW 16:26

Why SPIN Leads to Sin

Why does SPIN lead to sin? What else can result from living life out of its current season, with priorities in radical need of balance combined with isolation from others and neglect of your own soul care? When life is spinning for me, I have a tendency to be quick-tempered and on edge. I say things I shouldn't say, with an energy that should be reserved for a baseball coach talking to an umpire about a play that didn't go his way at home plate in the bottom of the ninth. I am irritable and short on patience. I get excessively rigid in my thinking and extend less grace to others when they need it the most. I gossip more, argue more, accuse more and generally feel like a dog chasing its tail.

When life starts moving too fast because of an overloaded calendar, I have a tendency to live in an almost perpetual state of stress and general uneasiness. I don't think any of us are easy to live with when we are in a hurry to get things done and don't have any recuperation time built into our lives. Now that I think about it, SPIN not only leads to sin, it *is* sin!

In short, we try to *do* instead of *be*. We become human *doings* and cease to be human *beings*. Yes, I understand stuff has to get done; but when we spend all of our time doing the things that we think *have* to get done—in the world, at church, at the office—life becomes out of balance and less enjoyable. We miss things that are important to see, feel or smell when we are moving too fast.

For example, if you are driving here in California, especially along the coastline with its amazing views of the Pacific Ocean, the beaches, palm trees and cliffs, you can miss all the beauty the journey can provide if you are simply going from point A to point B as fast as you can. You miss the beauty and grace of the waves, or the sunset glistening off the water and the color it produces as it sinks below the horizon. Do you often neglect things of beauty that add value to your life because you are more enamored with the destination than the journey?

I will be the first to raise my hand and say, that's me. Why do I need to see the waves or a sunset? What value can they add to my life? I have a to-do list I need to finish, and I really like the feeling that work and accomplishment give me.

Perhaps we could all pace ourselves to enjoy the journey along the way . . . to pause and breathe in all that the journey has to offer. I'm not talking about a vacation here; I'm talking about daily life—pausing daily to enjoy what's going on around us.

When life starts to spin faster and faster, we can miss important occasions or appointments, like a friend's birthday, a dental appointment, a child's soccer game or an anniversary. And the unexpected—things that just happen—really floor us because we don't have time to deal with them. Or what about those unpleasant things that only exacerbate a hurried and hectic life—things like a flat tire or the flu or maybe an added project at work?

The Drift of Neglect

To neglect means to pay little or no attention to, or even have a disregard for, someone or something. Neglect happens because we are not paying attention to what's going on around us or we are paying too much attention to the wrong things or wrong people—like the people at work instead of the people at home. Neglect is unknowingly drifting away from what is important.

I don't know if you have ever been in a canoe without a paddle. I have. A calm lake combined with a warm day and a quiet environment equals a nap, amen? I can remember a camp where I worked for a summer. They had canoes and "canoe time" for staff only. When all the camp attendees had left and the camp was relatively empty, you could grab a canoe, a paddle, a couple of life vests (one for a pillow) and row out to a quiet place. There were no anchors in the canoes, so you couldn't ground yourself in the middle of the lake or in one certain place. You had two choices. Paddle . . . or drift. You could keep paddling to get to where you wanted and pull up your canoe on the shore, or you could stop paddling and drift.

On a particularly beautiful day, while working at a camp tucked in the mountains of Southern California, I went out for my canoe ride. I paddled out to an area of the lake, situated the paddle on the floor of the boat, took the extra life vest and propped it up near one end of the canoe and gently placed my head upon it. The gentle rocking of the lake combined with heavy eyes and a tired body put me to sleep.

After an hour or so, I woke up to noise, chaos and commotion. I quickly sat up to see what was going on. I felt disoriented. My surroundings had changed, the landscape had changed, there were people around me playing and splashing, and there were other canoes. Where was I? What happened? Drift happened. I couldn't see it as I paddled out, but it was there. The subtle current and gentle wind had moved me from where I was to where I didn't want to be. I had worked hard—paddled hard to get to where I wanted to be, then fell asleep. When I woke up, I was in a completely different location.

The same is true with spiritual drift. When you neglect the current and wind around you, you can wind up in a surprising or even dangerous place when you finally realize it. Sometimes you become undermined by the current of busyness and tragically end up in the wrong place, unaware of how you got there. In other words, time + the current = drift into the wrong place. You never drift into the right place; you must paddle there.

Soul care—practicing correct priorities and accountability—comes with a paddle. It requires action, not passivity. The enemy of this world keeps a subtle and underlying current of busyness and a gentle wind of accomplishment around you until you wake up one day and say, "Where am I?" My friend, you have been sleeping; you have neglected to pay attention to the warning signs around you.

Gordon MacDonald wrote, "Our public worlds are filled with a seeming infinity of demands upon our time, our loyalties, our money, and our energies."[1] It is true: God loves us, and everyone else has a wonderful plan for our life. As a result, we must be active when it comes to our spiritual health. It can feel like a constant struggle to ignore all the good opportunities that come our way.

Let's face it, most of these opportunities aren't bad, they just take time—time we don't have if we want to stay healthy. We only have 24 hours in each day. If we overload that time, even with really good things, it can work against us. We get in that current of busyness and drift to unhealthy places.

Did you ever notice that when you feel hurried you often stop doing the things you should be doing, like spending time working on your inner or private life, or your relationship with Christ, or going to church, or serving others? You may even think that when you drop those things, your life will get easier. Not true! When you stop doing those things, other less-important tasks will fill up that time. Just ask people who don't know Jesus and see if their lives are flowing along in a leisurely fashion. Their lives are just as hectic as yours. Simply cutting out such things as a daily quiet time, going to church or serving others will not bring a level of balance to your life. In fact, the Bible says that reverence for God adds hours to each day (see Prov. 10:27).

Marriage Drift

It's ironic that Mary and I are writing this portion of the book on July 26, which just happens to be our twentieth anniversary. Over the course of our marriage, there were times when we both thought we weren't going to make it. After talking with several friends and acquaintances who also thought they weren't going to make it, we started to see a pattern. We call it the "V" of marital drift. It's what happened to us. As we have shared this concept with others, there seems to be a common thread or pattern that people recognize in their own life. "Yes," they say, "that's what happened to us," or "That is what's happening to us." The interesting thing about the "V" of marital drift is that you can see where you are, where you have been and, most importantly, where you could potentially be headed.

When I proposed to Mary more than 21 years ago, life was much simpler. Although we thought life was tough, there weren't as many moving parts. Yes, I still managed to work too much, but for the most part, it was simple. We didn't argue as much, and we enjoyed life and each other. Over time, we drifted apart. As it turns out, that phrase, "we drifted apart," seems to resonate with others, not only to those who are in ministry, but also to those who are in the marketplace. Why do couples who passionately said yes at the altar on their wedding day find themselves struggling to keep their marriage alive 10, 15, 20 years later? For us it was neglect. I (Craig) say "us" because we are a couple. However, most of the issues were started and furthered by me. I neglected to nurture my relationship with my wife, and over time, the relationship deteriorated.

The nature of the "V" is that the opening at the top of the letter expands over time and separates itself from the base. In this case, the "V" shows the separation of a relationship over time. When you get married, you are together, on the same page, in sync—you are at the bottom of the "V" and you are happy! But, if you neglect your relationship over time, the natural tendency is to drift apart. A subtle wedge begins to appear and the "V" widens a bit, but not too much. It's a lower case "v." *There is no need to get worried at this point,* you think to yourself. But you know it takes work to stay together and stay relationally connected. It takes work to stay healthy. If you don't actively make changes to connect and build on your relationship, the lowercase "v" will turn into a capital "V," and you will continue to separate from each other and pull apart. Let's take a look at how this works.

Happy Together

On July 26, 1991, Mary and I said the words "I do." They were words of commitment and resolve. We had dated each other for almost eight years. Mary was the one for me and I was the one for her. We enjoyed each other's company and had fun together. We thought about ways to show each other how much we loved and valued our relationship. We set time aside for each other. We remembered special occasions and celebrated crazy anniversaries like our first date at Disneyland. We made song mixes for each other, wrote love messages on puzzle pieces and stayed out late kissing, talking and sharing our deepest thoughts and dreams with each other. We were in love. Yes, all three Greek words for "love."

Dreams and Disillusionment

While Mary was finishing graduate school, I had already started working at a great church. As with any church, I was given some occasional opportunities as I implemented programs and changed existing ones; but for the most part, people liked the changes. I had a great team of people who helped launch and expand ministry, and I experienced success in a relatively short time.

Let me define the word "success" as I use it here. Numbers were going up! Attendance numbers were going up; volunteer numbers were going up; energy and enthusiasm were going up. It was awesome! I started to spend more time at church and invest more of myself there because lives were being changed. I had *dreams* of making the world a better place. I wasn't being told to do more; I *wanted* to do more. I liked what I was doing. I would finish the day at church and go home to work . . . on church. If you haven't guessed it by now, church wasn't 9:00 to 5:00. It was 9:00 to 9:00, 24/7.

Mary and I started to have conversations almost immediately about how my time was being spent. The conversations exhausted me. I would leave for church to pursue *dreams* to later return home to a *disillusioned* wife who desperately wanted to spend time with her husband. It became an immediate source of contention in our marriage. Our time together became more combative than collaborative, and the number 1 topic of dissension was how I was spending my time and how she felt like she wasn't a priority to me. Mary was becoming a married widow. I spent all my energy trying to advance my dreams, leaving no energy for her when I got home. The goal of expanding ministry trumped the disillusionment of marriage, and the "V" began to expand.

I (Mary) remember, early in our marriage, realizing that I didn't have a clue what to do to bring us closer together. I started to pick up books on marriage I thought could help us and would read them to look for a quick fix or a suggestion that would turn our relationship around or stop the drift. In the first year of our marriage, I read a book that suggested writing out a list of the 10 qualities that attracted you to your mate and then to take that list and read it at the beginning of the day, each day. The idea was to focus on the positive aspects of the other person's character and make a choice to see the good qualities, not the bad ones. I remember doing that exercise, and it prevented me from running out the door when things got rough. I stayed in the marriage, but I was definitely disillusioned when my dreams didn't come true immediately and my expectations of marriage were largely unmet in those years.

Important and Insignificant

People typically have a tendency to gravitate to where they feel significant and valued. I (Craig) was no exception to that. At work I felt important because others were telling me that I *was* making a difference. I was being encouraged. I cast vision, and as a team we all carried out that vision.

Contrast that with my life at home where Mary was asking me to help out around the house more and do what I thought were menial tasks like laundry and taking out the trash or changing a diaper. Mary wasn't telling me how great I was, and she wasn't listening to my every whim with a smile on her face—mostly because she was overworked at home and I was under-involved. Reality was, she wasn't telling me I was great because I *wasn't* great at home. I wasn't even trying to be great at home.

I began to feel more important at the office and insignificant at home. It felt like I was always in trouble when I came home from work. I used to joke with Mary that I wanted her to meet me at the door like our golden retriever. Holiday would always be so happy to see me no matter how late I came in the door that her tail would wag hard enough to move her whole body. Mary would reply, "Come home at 5:00 PM, and I will be *that* happy to see you!"

Important and *insignificant* in the home is a different thing altogether for the person who has chosen to give up a career in order to stay home with the kiddos. I (Mary) used to feel important and valued in my job as a school speech therapist before I had kids. I also felt in control of my environment. I had lesson plans and a schedule, and I was off from work at 3:00 each day. But a mom is never off work, and you never know what a day, or night, for that matter, will bring with kids.

Our twin boys were born prematurely. Cameron had feeding problems and was diagnosed with "failure to thrive" at six months of age. He had his first surgery at eight months, followed by years of occupational therapy and specialist doctor visits, almost all of which I went to alone with another baby in tow. When he was three and a half, he had a serious injury resulting in immediate blindness in his right eye and years of rehabilitation and surgeries.

Of course, I was *needed* and important at home. Of course, I was *significant* to my children. But what about feeling needed by, and significant to, my husband? I felt insignificant to him when he never came home from work on time to eat dinner with us. I felt insignificant because date nights were routine and not romantic, planned-in-advance events. I felt insignificant mostly because I ranked at the bottom of the priority list. It felt like I got the leftovers in the doggie bag after Craig had gone to eat at a five-star restaurant. I didn't want the leftover emotions from a stressful day at work. I wanted an attentive husband and daddy to take over when he walked in the door.

If you are in this pattern of feeling important somewhere other than home and insignificant when you are at home, you begin to think, *I don't deserve to be treated like this. This isn't what I signed up for. Others treat me better than my wife (or husband).*

Exciting and Exhausting

When this kind of thinking and self-talk starts to happen, the drift is well underway in your marriage. Soon you will find yourself making choices to be in the environment that's exciting. Work life seems to be easier to navigate than home life. There is a unique energy there, more passion, fewer arguments and disagreements. Work almost seems to energize you, so you spend more time there. You have come to love your work environment rather than your home environment. I (Craig) am writing from experience. I get it. I understand. I would leave the office at night to go home to a mentally and emotionally taxing environment, and the kicker is that I was the biggest contributor to the exhausting environment there.

Craig and I used to spend our Fridays together. That was his day off from church and we would start it by going out to breakfast after dropping the kids off at school. Our favorite spot is in Laguna Beach, overlooking the cliffs, where they make your favorite omelet to order as part of a delicious buffet. Usually, our day would start off well but then as we got out our calendars and began to talk through the upcoming week, conflict would quickly develop. "How many nights a week are you going to be out?" I would ask. To which he would respond by asking me to join him at different church events so he would see the kids before bedtime. Notoriously, he would call his assistant or someone on his team to check in on "a few things" while we were together on his day off, and I would quickly become impatient and frustrated. There was no excitement in our time together. It was exhausting because it was a constant battle between home time and work time.

It was nearly impossible to detach my husband from his job, even for one day a week. Just talking to him about the schedule was exhausting. Don't get me wrong. Not every Friday was like this. But as time went on, we had more battles on Friday than any other day of the week, because that was the day we spent together. And we each thought we knew how that day should go. All the other days of the week I was in charge at home and he was in charge at work. But on Fridays, the battle for control reared its ugly head.

At this point in your marriage neglect, you may begin to make choices to not be at home at all or not connect. You may find that you have drifted in the opposite direction of home and family life and eventually wake up to find yourself in a place you never meant to go.

Desired and Detached

The pattern is to move away from pain and conflict and gravitate to where you are wanted and needed. You may feel that when you are at home there is constant turmoil and disagreement that takes more and more energy. You feel like you're living on a hamster wheel of discontent. You want to be somewhere else, *anywhere* else, where you feel loved and valued, where you feel wanted, needed and desired.

As you continue to drift away from home and away from your spouse, you start drifting toward something else. It may be the office and work. It may be toward another person who shows a desire to be with you. Maybe it's a neighbor, a person at the gym, an old boyfriend or girlfriend you have recently "reconnected" with on Facebook. It might even be someone in your small group who pays more attention to you than your spouse does. This person may be a better listener, a smarter dresser, a more romantic spouse or maybe even a terrific parent. Whatever is missing in your relationship with your spouse will seemingly be there with the other person. Where your spouse is "suddenly all wrong," the other person is "suddenly all right." And, as the devil would have it, that person feels the same way about you.

You may even feel so detached from your spouse that you rationalize the desire you feel toward someone else because you believe you have a "right to be happy." You may even begin to believe the lie that you "never really loved your spouse" and you shouldn't have married him or her in the first place. Or you might believe the lie that there's nothing wrong being "best friends" with a person of the opposite sex if you haven't crossed the line sexually. Satan blurs the line between right and wrong, and before you know it, you may find yourself in a compromising position. You start telling little white lies to your spouse about where you have been and what you have been doing, and you begin thinking, *What they don't know won't hurt them*. But of course you know deep down that it will.

It's the law of drift. If you are drifting away from one thing, you are drifting toward another; and in this world where our enemy's influence is strong, you never drift into a healthy situation. You always drift where the current is taking you; and if you are in a canoe without a paddle, you are in trouble.

I don't believe any married man or woman wakes up one day and says, out of the blue, "I'm going to have an affair today." You never stand at the altar on your wedding day and say, "In about seven years, it will be time to have an inappropriate relationship." No, these things happen as a result of neglect after the wedding day. What we did as boyfriend and girlfriend while dating, we stopped doing when we became husband and wife. The romance we shared, the beauty we observed, the love notes we wrote, the time we spent pursuing each other have all but left the relationship.

You can recall those days, can't you? The impromptu dinners, the picnics, the four-hour phone conversations. I can remember when Mary and I didn't have two nickels to rub together while we were dating. If I was away on a trip, or speaking somewhere, I would call from a pay phone. Yes, there used to be phones you could walk up to, put money in and call someone. Well, I would call her and let the phone ring once and then hang up. It wasn't a cruel joke; it was my way of letting her know that I was thinking about her even though I didn't have the money to talk to her. When I would hang up, the pay phone would return the money and I could call her again a few hours later. That's how it is when you are dating. But over time, if you fail to pursue romance with your spouse, you will drift apart. This happens when you neglect to nurture your relationship with that person.

Neglect is a part of SPIN—it's the last letter in the acronym. Neglect is part of a workaholic personality. When life seems to be spinning faster and faster, you can be sure that neglect is part of your most important relationships.

You may not have intentionally said, "Okay, it's time to stop all those nurturing things we did before we were married," but at some point, you stopped paddling, and the current took you to a place you never intended to be. Over time you drifted away from your home and embraced work or outside relationships. If things don't change, you grow complacent as a couple until one day you are being served divorce papers or told by your spouse that it's over. *Or* you find your wife's journal and realize that you have fallen asleep in the canoe of your marriage and you've drifted far away from your starting point.

That's how our enemy uses drift. There is a Niagara Falls drop at the end; but by the time you wake up, you are already over the edge and no life vest will keep you afloat, no amount of paddling will get you back to where you started. You will go over the edge. You will crash. You will die.

BUT, death is part of God's process. Just ask Lazarus and the others there that day when Jesus raised him from death to life. In other words, there is life after the *falls* . . . after all of them.

SECTION 2

LEARNING

STOP

5

SLOW DOWN

I'm in a hurry to get things done, oh I rush and rush until life's no fun.

ALABAMA

Busy . . . How About You?

I love to keep busy. I feel guilty if I am not doing something. Call me a driven, type A firstborn or only child. I don't care. Give me something to do or else I'll create something to do. Rest is not only hard for me, but it also feels impossible.

When I see someone I haven't seen in a while, I usually ask a question and, in turn, I usually get the same question volleyed back to me. "How are you doing?" The typical response is, "Great. Busy. How about you?" For some reason, we not only like to keep busy, but we also like to tell others about it.

Since I have started to pay a bit more attention, I think my reason for the "busy" answer is to validate how hard a worker I am. In some way, I've connected my self-esteem to how much work I output on a daily basis. I feel more important when I am busy. I feel like I can better justify my existence. I also feel that if I am busier than the next person, have more projects on the table, I am more successful in others' eyes. Sick, I know, but true.

With that in mind, and after four years of trying to recalibrate the pace of my life, I went mindfully into a group of people I hadn't seen in a long time. I knew the question would come up immediately, and it did. The first person I ran into said, "Hey, Craig, how you doing?" And then he put the busy question right on a tee for me. "You been busy?" I could feel a strong desire to say, "Shoot, I have been so busy lately it's not even funny," but I didn't. I fought every emotional piece of energy in my mind and body and said, "No, not real busy . . . trying to be more balanced."

Time stopped, the matrix was on. The other person didn't know how to respond. We were both in uncharted water. Now what? Usually this was all preprogrammed. I had violated the first unwritten rule of I-haven't-seen-you-in-a-while-what-have-you-been-up-to etiquette. The response I received back was, "Oh, good," and then he walked away, and I stood there an emotional basket case.

Why was I feeling this flood of emotion over a minute's conversation? I figured it out immediately. I was worried this guy was going to work his way around the room with people he hadn't seen in a while and follow the correct protocol and tell everyone that he is busy and then ask everyone if they are busy. Then there would be a pause and he would say, "I saw Craig over there a few minutes ago, and he isn't busy at all. He said something about balance. Slacker! Unproductive sloth! Who does he think he is? We are over here working our rear ends off and he is living balanced?"

Before we can find balance, we need to find out the root of *why* we need balance. We do not have unlimited resources. Our batteries run out over time depending on how much we use them. Even though my wife called me the Energizer Bunny, I couldn't go forever without recharging. Just like my laptop. I am sitting here writing this book on my Mac. There is an icon in the upper right-hand corner of the screen that shows a battery symbol. It starts out with a full charge, but eventually a convenient little reminder will pop up on my computer screen that says, "You are now running on reserve power." It's actually a nice little reminder. It lets me know in a subtle way that it will be necessary very soon to plug my computer cord into a power source.

There are times when I wish I were as authentic as my computer. I wish I could simply acknowledge that I'm out of power and, if I don't get plugged in soon, I'm going to die right here. I really like this analogy, so let me beat on it some more. To this date, I have never seen my computer get up and walk over and plug itself into an electrical outlet. I have to plug it in. The computer needs help. We all need some help.

I have found that the more programs I have open on the computer, the more work I do, the brighter the screen burns and the faster the power is used up. If I choose to continue to work on the computer, open more programs, keep the screen burning at its optimum brightness, at some point the computer will no longer warn me; it will simply shut off. My computer doesn't care what I think of it. It just knows it needs power, and if it doesn't get it, it's going to shut off.

When I am unwilling to ask others for help or I'm too proud to ask for help, it would be great if I had a simple indicator that could be seen by some dear friend who would say, "Craig, we need to get you plugged in. It looks like you are running out of power." I know that will never be a reality, but if you look closely, you will see when some people are running low. Here are five warning signs that a person is on reserve power.

1. Physical tiredness
2. Irritability
3. Lack of patience with others
4. Withdrawal from friends or family
5. Desire for control

I often don't notice these warning signs when they are present in me. I must rely on Mary or others to tell me I need to recharge, plug in and stay healthy.

I'm not only talking about plugging in spiritually. I am also talking about plugging in emotionally, intellectually and physically. We need to recharge body, soul and spirit. I don't want to understate the healthiness of your spiritual life and walk, but I want you to be aware that you must allow your body and mind, as well as your heart, to plug in and get recharged too.

Compassion Fatigue

Can doing more good bring more bad? The unfortunate yet simple answer is yes. There is even a name for it—*compassion fatigue*. Can we care too much? I like what good friend and Marriage and Family Counselor Jill Catuara says: "Technically, we can't care too much, but we can use our caring for others to avoid caring for those who God wants us to care for first, namely our own families." We rarely get praise from others for being a good spouse or parent, but we often get praise for what we are doing in our job.

Furthermore, when your job has such a focus on others that you often neglect your own soul care, you are in danger of developing destructive be-haviors, addictions and attitudes.

The Gospel narrative in Mark 6 is descriptive of people in ministry or caring professions. Note that Jesus usually sought solitude or time alone with His close friends or His heavenly Father after intense bursts of min-istry or when difficulty and discouragement came His way. Mark 6 shares one of those times. Jesus had just received news from His apostles about the death of John the Baptist. It was after this news that Jesus decided it was time for a retreat; it was time to get away. Jesus says in Mark 6:31: "Let's get away from the crowds for a while and rest." I like the narrative Mark gives after he records Jesus' words in the same verse. He says, "There were so many people coming and going that Jesus and his apostles didn't even have time to eat." Have you ever felt that way—too busy to eat? Me too. The disciples were busy, and they didn't even have email or cell phones! They could get into a boat, get away, and they wouldn't get a call or a text message.

The narrative continues as Jesus and the apostles shove off in the boat so they can rest from the crowds and refill their tanks. They must have thought, *Yes! Ministry is done; everyone is gone! I'm tired!* As they sailed away from shore, I can see one of the exhausted sailors squinting as he looked back. Rubbing his tired eyes in an effort to get a better focus, he says,

"What?! Is that . . . is the . . . umm, Jesus, why is the crowd running along the shore? Are they . . . are they following us?" I wonder how Jesus responded. He knew there was more ministering to people ahead. I wish I could have been there in that moment to capture the nonverbal communication or the dialogue, or perhaps feel the tension as everyone sat in silence after that socially awkward apostle vented.

Mark 6:33 records the simple fact that the crowd was indeed following the boat. They were running along the shore's edge, watching the boat and trying to mentally gauge where it would land. The crowd got it right. The narrative goes on to tell us that the group got there ahead of Jesus and His apostles.

You can relate, can't you? No matter how hard you try to get away to rest, there is someone who needs help, or you simply can't let go. The crowd followed Jesus' boat, and they will follow your church or ministry. Jesus had compassion for people; I often have a tendency to get frustrated with them. I sometimes say, "Wouldn't ministry be easy if there were no people?" But there are people, and long-term ministry isn't easy.

How does this fit with compassion fatigue? Because ministry never stops, the natural assumption is that we should never stop.

We have already dedicated some time to addressing the seasons of life and where our time should be spent during those seasons. From a workaholic personality's point of view and experience, in ministry there are no seasons. We say things like, "We're just in a busy season right now" or "When things slow down, I will take some time off." If you haven't already guessed it, you will always be in a busy season and things won't slow down until you die. Until that time, if you want to make a case for seasons in ministry, the only two I am aware of are busy and busier.

What starts out as compassion morphs into compulsion. Care and compassion shown to others is not where we get sideways; it's the addiction to such things that gets us into burnout trouble. I'm not sure if it's because we don't think others can do what we are doing, or if we are control freaks or just have a compassion addiction. But something is slightly left of center when it comes to doing too much. And it's usually all good stuff! On some level, it's like the person who suffers from Obsessive Compulsive Disorder. Washing your hands is a good thing; but washing your hands over and over until your skin is raw is unhealthy.

Mark 6:34 tells us, "A vast crowd was there as he stepped from the boat, and he had compassion on them because they were like sheep without a shepherd. So he taught them many things." I used to justify my worka-holic lifestyle with this verse. I would say, "Jesus went from one thing to an-other. You can't schedule meeting the needs of others on a calendar. What if someone needs my help? What if I need to be at all those meetings? Those people need me." Yes, I understand how you can leverage that verse into more work, but let's look at Jesus' life in context with His season. Was He married? Did He have family responsibilities? Were His wife and kids waiting for Him at home? No. His season was "single, no children"; there-fore, He didn't have outside responsibilities to His family.

The first part of learning STOP is to take your foot off the gas. When you stop what powers your workaholic life, at least you aren't speeding ahead any longer. Your foot may not have fully transferred to the brake, and that's okay. You can take one pedal at a time.

I have found that what usually happens is that we learn to drive with both feet. After Mary and I would *talk* about my schedule, I would keep one foot on the gas and the other foot on the brake. This would give the appearance of slowing down, but I could continue to accelerate without coming to a complete stop. In other words, when Mary was content that my foot was on the brake, and she was happy I was making progress, life would return to normal. The only thing this accomplished was a false hope for Mary and new brakes for me, which I would wear out again and again.

Because of my relentless stubbornness, I had to come to the end before I could begin again. How about you? Can doing more good be wrong?

Multi-taskmaster

If you are a mom or a wife (and you have to be *all things to all people*), you have to multitask, don't you? If we didn't, how would we drive the carpool and quiz the kids on spelling words while applying our makeup and listen-ing to the weather forecast? Or my (Mary's) personal favorite: help the kids with homework while making dinner, setting the table and talking on the phone to my mom. I'll admit it. I'm a happy multi-tasker. I pride myself in my ability to do several things at once.

I love to be on my iPhone checking Facebook, email, texting friends or playing games. Most days at work as a school speech therapist I would spend lunchtime inside my classroom, not in the teacher's lounge. I'd use that time to finish a report, talk to Craig on the phone and eat a granola bar, because you can eat a bar and not stop working. I loved it when the students would come to my room to play games during their lunchtime, but that translated into more for me to pay attention to at the same time. This allowed no downtime on my 45-minute lunch and left me scrambling to get to the restroom before the bell rang and my next session began.

By the time I left for home, I would be exhausted and actually looked forward to a bit of alone time in the car. The sad part was that I never really felt like I had accomplished enough in my time at work. I felt a constant nagging that I didn't get through my daily checklist. There was actually no possible way that I *could* get through the list, but I made it anyway. Every day I would carry over to the next day the things that didn't get done. The only day of the year that I would actually finish my work was the last day of school.

I found out that I am not alone in this world of perpetual motion when I posted this question on Facebook: "What does multitasking look like to you?" A close friend of mine answered, "Grading papers while making dinner and helping kids with homework and loading laundry and feeding the dog, and it all has to overlap or it doesn't get done."

Another friend said, "Sleeping and mulling over the next day's lesson plans at the same time." Can anyone relate to that? Trying to sleep, yet your overloaded, stressed-out brain won't shut down, so you just keep working in your mind while you sleep. A friend answered my post like this:

> Rushing to the house from work, grabbing one kid to go to practice, asking another kid to take stuff out of the freezer for dinner, back into the car, call fellow moms to set up carpool schedule, drop off the one in the car for practice, read emails at the red lights while grabbing another kid plus carpooling kids from high school practice, take them all home, go back to first kid's practice while on the phone with insurance company or some other household-related task, go home, make dinner while reviewing schedule with family, then head back out for midweek Bible study or Scouts, buy groceries or go to Target while waiting to pick up kids. Come home, then help with homework and play a few "Words with Friends" and then hit the hay.

I feel tired just reading that! However, just because we are all doing it doesn't mean it's good for us. We may go so far as to say: "If I don't multitask life in my world, it will stop." Believe me, I understand. But after looking at the research, both Craig and I are trying to single-task more. There is some significant research that suggests multitasking is (hold your breath) bad for us.

So what is multitasking? Multitasking is engaging in two or more activities at the same time. Balancing the checkbook online while texting a friend and returning email. When we multitask, our brain jumps around from item to item, and according to Dr. Archibald Hart, that "is not only ineffective for learning, but many scientists are now saying it also produces significant stress."[1] Further research from Dr. Hart reveals that "a high level of multiprocessing and simultaneous multisensory inputting has destructive effects on the pleasure system of the brain."[2]

I know that after engaging in multitasking for a long period of time, it's hard for me to shut down. I get jittery and have trouble sitting still. My mind goes to unfinished work, and if there is even a slight lull in the conversation, I think to myself, *Check your phone. Maybe something is happening there that I can do.* A high level of multitasking also has destructive effects on relationships. My ability to multitask and my inability to relax have hurt those I love the most. I have had uncomfortable conversations with Craig about the fact that I tend to be on my phone texting or checking emails, even when I am out with him on a date night. Even close friends have been hurt by my not shutting down to be present in the moment when we are just hanging out.

After digging a little deeper, I found that multitasking was originally used as a computing term. It wasn't until the 1990s that the term was applied to people. The thing is, computers don't have feelings, carpools or kids. However, when a computer is doing more than it was designed for, it does one of two things: either (1) it freezes up—Mac users, can I get a "beach ball of death" amen—or worse, (2) it crashes—PC users, can I . . . oh never mind. It's interesting that too much multitasking, even on computers, can lead to lockups, freezes or even crashes. I believe the same is true with people.

Think of all the advancement in technology within our lifetime. Just a few years back, no one had a cell phone. To reach someone urgently, you could call their pager and then wait for them to find a pay phone to call you back. Contrast that with today, when even our elementary kids have smart phones, iPads, Facebook accounts, laptops and handheld electronics that allow them to connect wirelessly to the Web, instant message and text friends, and maybe even start a flash mob.

Isn't it ironic that we are more "connected" than ever with the help of our electronics, yet we may have no idea what is really going on in our kids' lives? What happened to the family bike ride or picnic? Kids today are more stimulated than ever, yet they are quick to say they are bored. It's as if we feel that if we are not constantly keeping our children engaged in some sort of "betterness program," whether it's sports, music, tutoring or even church activities, then we are bad parents for wasting their developing minds. And we certainly don't want to look like a bad parent. After all, everyone else is busy shuttling their kids around every night of the week, so why shouldn't we? But is this really the best thing for our kids? Is it the best thing for our families?

I've been in education for more than 20 years, and what I've noticed is that kids need less "screen time" and more "face time" with their family. In our home, that is a difficult thing to convince the kids of, and sometimes difficult to convince the big kid too. But we have observed that the more video games our kids play, the more difficult they are to get along with and the quicker they are bored in social settings. We have to make a conscious effort to tell the kids to shut off the screens and go outside and play, as well as a conscious effort to build in meaningful conversations with them at mealtimes.

Many years ago, no one had a watch but everyone had time. Today, everyone has a watch but no one has time. We have lost the ability to shut down and reload. It is important for us as parents to model the right pace for our kids. We can do this by simply stopping all the busyness and playing with them, whether we shoot hoops at the park, play a simple board game or engage in pretend play activities. When I stop and do this with my kids, they open up and start sharing things with me that I didn't know. I have found out about friends at school and stories that teachers have shared as well as problems their friends are having. My kids won't share these things when I am rushing around or not giving them the time they need. Sometimes I have to coax it out of them in an atmosphere of safety and calm. I hear these stories when we are one on one in the car or taking a walk on the trail. And there is nothing that recharges my batteries more than a good conversation!

Another way that we can model slowing down and reduce our multitasking lives is by shutting off the screens in the house and reading a book. It's tough to shut off the television, computer, handheld electronics and phone, but the rewards are worth it! Our family enjoys watching a few weekly shows together. Tuesday night in our home is family night. I bake some kind of yummy dessert, or the kids make popcorn, and we head to the family room for a night of laughter and entertainment. We all look forward to this night. The kids get their homework done early and we don't plan anything else on that night. This is one way that we slow down as a family.

Another way we do this is by having a regular nightly routine with our kids. From the time the kids were babies, we would spend the last 15 to 20 minutes of the day with them, reading books, praying with them and tucking them into bed. As they got older, we graduated from reading board books like *Barnyard Dance* to chapter books like the *Chronicles of Narnia*. This was precious slowing down time, and it not only helped us bond as a family, but it also helped our kids relax and unwind before bed. They fell asleep faster, with fewer trips to the kitchen and bathroom, after we said goodnight.

In summer time, when the days are longer, we like to go for bike rides or walks on the trail after dinner. Building some of these "slow down" routines into your family life will model rest to your kids and will recharge your own batteries. As technology increases our ability to be "online" at all times, we need to make a potential parenting switch to help our kids understand the importance of *pause, stop* and *silent rest*. Their generation is one of speed and entertainment, and it's important to help them understand and value the almost lost art of meditation.

As I was reflecting on multitasking and people, I realized that some of my favorite people to hang out with are not people who multitask. My sister, Sherry, is a great example of a person who knows how to slow down and have fun. I love to be with her! She finds beauty all around her, and she enjoys it. Sherry doesn't wear a watch; she's on her own time schedule. She will often stop her car and get out to pick a beautiful flower. She has been known to carry a small shovel in her car and even stop to dig up a wildflower to replant at her home.

Recently, when I was visiting her, we planned a breakfast date on the island where she lives. After picking me up, she drove to the beach and unpacked a picnic basket complete with a beautiful apron, tablecloth and candle. She proceeded to cook me eggs and bacon on the beach grill, and we sat and enjoyed the view and each other's company. I felt valued and loved. My friend, Debbie, is another wonderful example of someone who doesn't multitask. When I asked her about it, she said:

I can't multitask very well at all, which is why I can't get as much done in a day as you can. In fact, the joke around my house is that I can't even talk on the phone and do something else, which is actually true. If I'm talking to someone, I usually sit down and focus on the conversation. If I try to do laundry or empty the dishwasher, or anything, I can't concentrate on what we are talking about; but since I can't, I try to focus on the positive, which is to try to do whatever thing I am doing at the moment well—especially when it comes to people and listening to them or being with them. No wonder I enjoy being with her!

The more I learn about multitasking, the more I realize it's not necessarily something I should be bragging about. Slowing down means being present in the moment and doing one thing well. It means relating to others by looking them in the eye, giving them my full attention and showing them that, at that moment, they are the most important and valuable person in the world to me.

6

THINK AHEAD

When values are clear, decisions are easy.

ROY DISNEY

Wherever You Go, There You Are

I (Craig) usually held team meetings at our home or one of my team members' homes. I preferred the informal environment. We would typically meet from 9:00 to 12:00 every other Monday and do what most teams do during their meetings. We would go over items that just needed to get done, connect relationally over lunch and then talk about where we were headed as a ministry and as a team.

I don't care too much for details and to-do lists. I'm not very good at them and lose interest quickly. I prefer to talk about what's next, discuss the impossible, cast vision! "Vision"—the word itself suggests movement and is future oriented. My heart starts pumping harder just thinking about it. Vision isn't limited or stifled by details or specifics. Vision doesn't involve steps or constructs; it's more liquid and free. It's creative, moving forward, fun. Vision incites people to action. We even have a Bible verse for it: "Where there is no vision, the people perish" (Prov. 29:18, *KJV*).

I love to cast vision. I do so with all the excitement, energy and enthusiasm of a golden retriever puppy. When I used this verse from Proverbs, I would see people come alive when I started to tell them about the direction in which we were heading. Although I must admit, I would also see some people wilt under the barrage of enthusiasm I unleashed in those meetings. They didn't see me as a vision caster but as a vision blaster, relentlessly pushing them to more.

After a staff meeting one afternoon, I was on my way back to the office. I was excited about what we had talked about in the meeting—adding programs, doubling attendance, going to the next level. Energizing stuff! I decided to stop off at the local coffee shop for a grande nonfat caramel macchiato. Spurred on by a couple of extra shots of espresso, I came up with a few more ideas as I sipped my macchiato in the car and drove back to the office. I walked in holding my cup along with a napkin of freshly scribbled ideas I'd managed to write down between leaving the coffee shop and arriving at the office.

I noticed five of the women on the team huddled around a table in a room with the door closed. There were glass inserts in the office doors, so I could see them laughing and having a good time. I like laughing, so I thought I would just pop in and join the fun. My eyes were bright, my energy was high, and my smile was broad. I pushed open the door handle with the heel of my hand while still gripping my double-cupped caramel macchiato. As soon as the door opened the laughter stopped as if you had just pressed the pause button on your DVR. Time seemed to freeze . . . awkwardly. The joyful emotion that had just taken place in the room felt like it was sucked out with a powerful vortex when I opened the door. It felt as though I was the parent and the five people before me had been caught red-handed with their collective hand in the cookie jar.

Apparently, I had caught them by surprise. Surprises can be good. For example, when you have a birthday and a friend plans a party and doesn't let you know anything about it. He or she hides everything from you right up to the point you think your birthday has been forgotten. Suddenly, when you are completely off balance, you walk into a restaurant or a dark room and all the secret planning and anticipation come to a resounding blast as several people shout, "Surprise!" It's welcoming and powerful; you feel loved and valued and honored. These people gave up a lot to not only be there but to keep it all a secret. They want to see your reaction, your face, your surprise and your joy! Everyone laughs and smiles!

There are other surprises. They are the "caught you off guard" surprises. This was one of them. There I stood, with a waning half-smile and half a caramel macchiato that I suddenly had no desire to finish. One quick-minded person managed to choke out the words, "We were just talking about you." All the others nodded in agreement. "Come on in!" was the follow-up comment "Sit down."

"What were you guys talking about?" I asked.

"Oh, staff meeting . . . leadership stuff."

"No, seriously, what were you talking about?"

The verbal president in the room said they had been talking about my nickname.

What? A nickname . . . for me? Awesome! At that point, I lost all emotional awareness of the room and went straight to arrogance. I love nicknames. They are signs of endearment, closeness and a bond between friends. I poked, pleaded and prodded them to tell me, but they went from simply changing the subject to reluctance to outright obstinance. It was evident they were all going to remain tight-lipped about the name. In one last-ditch effort, I asked for a hint and was lucky enough to catch one of them napping, who blurted out, to the gasp of the others, "It's a cartoon character."

A cartoon character? Which one? There are so many cool cartoon characters. SpongeBob or Squidward? Garfield or Odie? George Jetson, Fred Flintstone, Inspector Gadget? I ran through the options, but I was thinking in the wrong place. I was thinking cool, relevant, loving. They, unfortunately, were not.

Because I had lost all emotional resonance with the vibe in the room, I could not read the emotion in their faces. If I could have read the room, I would have left. I was not thinking or seeing clearly, nor was I feeling the tension growing in the room. Finally, as if to put me out of my misery, someone said, "It's Taz. You know, the Tasmanian Devil?"

What? He didn't even make my list. Forget about the list, he never crossed my mind. *Why Taz?*

If you are not familiar with this Warner Brothers cartoon character, let me introduce you. Or if you do know who the Tasmanian Devil is, let me refresh your memory. The Tasmanian Devil does not speak. He grunts, makes noise and generally creates chaos. He is most known for simply spinning. When he travels from one place to the next, he spins. He does not walk, he does not jog, he does not run, he spins . . . violently. The comedic element to the Taz is that wherever he moves, he leaves a wake of destruction. If he bumps into a tree, it splinters. If he hits a rock, it explodes. Occasionally, he stops if someone is bold enough to stand in his destructive path, but he only stops for a brief moment because the Taz is all about movement. He disappears as fast as he appears. He spins in, then he spins out. And this, my friends, was my nickname.

Feeling sober, and in deep thought, I headed to my corner. Once I had a chance to think for a minute and organize my thoughts, I became a *Taz* bit angry. Who were they to call me Taz? I mean it was only five people's opinion. I'm sure not everyone felt this way. Perhaps this was a small faction and not a full representation of the team. Before making a rebuttal, I thought I would head over to our Empowering Kids and Orphan Impact offices. Still feeling a bit down, I sought encouragement from different team members. As I opened the door to the office, I was greeted by one of our most outgoing, tell-it-like-it-is, funny people on the team. Without missing a beat she said, "Taz Man."

What? Excuse me? "Taz Man?" *Are you kidding me? Did someone put her up to this? Is everyone going to jump out of a closet and say, "Surprise"?* No, apparently not.

I *was* "The Taz," spinning recklessly out of control, with regard for no one, not even myself. Hurrying the pace because people need Jesus. Adding more programs because we want to get bigger. Adding another service because people need to hear about Jesus. Yes, these are all great things, but they are not for one person, one church to do. Please understand, I loved ALL of it, and I wanted to do more. I was a children's pastor with 30 paid staff, a million-dollar budget and a guilt complex. I was CEO of Empowering Kids, Inc., Orphan Impact International, and I was also traveling a minimum of twice a month to speak at various conferences and churches.

I can recall Mary's and my first counseling appointment when Jim, our counselor, looked at me and asked, "Which of these things are you willing to give up?" And my response was, "I don't think I need to give up any of them. I can handle them all." Jim laughed; Mary sighed. I raised my hands, shrugged my shoulders and said, "What? I can." In counseling circles, I believe they call that denial.

Are You a Workaholic?

We work and work until we earn the label "workaholic"—a label some of us wear proudly. After all, workaholics, go-getters, entrepreneurs and overachievers are rewarded in life. I know that I was. Those people who arrive before work hours are seen as taking initiative, and those who stay late are seen as dedicated. They are the people who get advancements and bonuses, hugs and high fives, trophies and awards.

Listen, I don't want to squelch the positive traits of showing initiative, dedication and responsibility. I preach them to my kids and practice them myself. They are necessary life skills that should be taught, nurtured and modeled. It's the misuse, abuse and overuse of these traits that I am talking about. Simply examine your work habits in light of *your season*. Arriving early or staying late at your job may be necessary occasionally, but if you're doing this more than occasionally, burnout may be just around the corner.

There is a difference between being a hard worker and being a workaholic. The hard workers understand the limits of their season and maintain clear boundaries to avoid overwork. Workaholics have an addiction to work; and if you have an addiction to work, the problem is most likely twofold. First, you don't view overwork as an addiction, but rather as a leadership trait that should be rewarded and admired. Second, you probably don't know that your addiction isn't only hurting you; it most definitely is hurting those closest to you.

In chapter 3, I made the statement that all of us are messed up. We are sinful, fallen and broken, but redeemable! To me it feels like the work environment, in several areas, is broken and in need of redemption. It seems like the majority of work environments these days reward employees who are the most out of balance—those who are climbing the ladder of success and doing "whatever it takes" to get the job done.

There are many studies that confirm that workaholism is the source for many of our ailments today—not only emotionally, but mentally and physically as well. The word "workaholic" tells the story. It is combined from two words, "work" and "alcoholic," and paints a picture of addiction. Yet workaholism has almost become an admirable addiction in our society. We are praised and rewarded when we overwork.

It wasn't until I read Dr. Archibald Hart's book *Adrenaline and Stress* that I realized I wasn't just addicted to work but to my own adrenaline. I overworked because it felt good. The alcoholic takes the next drink because it feels good; the drug addict takes the next pill because it feels good; the workaholic takes the next appointment or opportunity because it feels good. Hart says, "We can get hooked on the pleasurable high that comes from the workings of the body's own defense system . . . and this addiction can control our actions and emotions."[1]

Adrenaline is usually released in our body to prepare us to cope with some type of impending stress. It gives us a sudden burst of energy. It's the classic fight, flight or freeze response. It minimizes pain, gives a feeling of power and is a natural "high." Adrenaline feels good. If you are a workaholic like me, it's almost certain that adrenaline addiction comes into play. Hard work has turned into overwork, which leads to an addiction. Just because the drug is coming from inside your body and not from outside of it doesn't mean you can't be addicted to it. I was completely unaware of why I created work for myself and took on more than I could handle. It was to create a fight, flight or freeze response so I could get the next rush of adrenaline.

The remedy, as prescribed by Jim, was to take six months off to detox my body and heal. No work for six months. You might be thinking, *That would be heaven.* But to an adrenaline addict, it's hell. Sometimes I would lie in bed and not want to get up. When I did go to our office, I couldn't think clearly; I couldn't create, write, cast vision or even formulate an idea. I experienced shakes, cold sweats, lack of appetite, rapid weight loss and depression—all of which lasted for several months. A vicious cycle is created when we overwork, release adrenaline, feel good, experience withdrawal, overwork, release adrenaline, feel good, experience withdrawal . . . and so on.

A vicious cycle is also created when your workaholic tendencies produce stress in your relationships. When the relationships closest to you

deteriorate and turn sour, you work more as a way to escape those sour relationships, which creates even more stress within the relationships. According to an article in the *New York Times*, "Most workaholics are either
perfectionists, have a need for control or a combination of both."[2] Workaholics become a virtual time bomb of stress. When people don't want to be
around us, we withdraw from them, and on and on the cycle goes.

According to Edmund Neuhaus, PhD, director of the Behavioral
Health Partial Hospital Program at McLean Hospital in Belmont, Massa-
chusetts, "If you're working to the exclusion of your family, your marriage,
other relationships, and your life is out of balance, or your physical health
is out of balance—when work takes an exclusive priority to everything else,
that's the more extreme end of the spectrum where it becomes a problem."[3]

Research does suggest that there is a general set of characteristics of
workaholics, and these characteristics were evident in my own life. Four
prominent characteristics for me were denial, poor self-esteem, obsessiveness and blame.

Denial

"I'm fine . . . all is well . . . I'm just a hard worker . . . I don't overwork . . .
my marriage is fine . . . I have lots of friends . . . I have balance . . . I'm not
irritable . . . I can let go." I used these phrases frequently, and I fully believed what I was saying. A person is usually the last one to know or admit
that he or she has a life balance issue.

I (Mary) would rationalize my workaholic patterns by saying things
like, "I'm not a workaholic; I'm just busy." "Of course, I'm busy, because I
have to wear several hats. I'm a pastor's wife, a mom, and a business owner,
so my roles are what keep me busy." "I can't stop doing any of these things
or they won't get done." "I *have* to do it all. I'm not choosing this. I don't
have a choice here."

Self-Esteem

Why self esteem? I (Craig) felt an inner drive to succeed that was beyond
rational ability. Call it what you want—choleric, type A, lionhearted, driven.
For me there was almost an inner voice saying, "If I can just pull off the
next event; if I can just write another book; if I can just get to the next level,
then life will be better. I will be better; all will be better than it is now."

It finally clicked for me when I started to help around the house. While
walking to the washing machine with a load of laundry, a little voice inside

me said, *Why are you doing this? This isn't what you were called to do. Why are you helping around the house?* I know this may upset the gals reading this book, but please hang in there with me for a moment. That little voice was present not only at the washing machine, but in just about every other area of my family's life. I didn't help out around the house, period. The root of this voice was the enemy himself fueling the fire of a self-esteem that was already suffering: "Craig, you take care of the important biblical stuff, and Mary can take care of the rest of the stuff at home." To be perfectly honest, I wasn't comfortable in my own skin.

All of that has changed over the last several years. I didn't *go* into the change; I had to *grow* into it. Realizing that Mary was doing life alone even when I was present was revealed to me while in counseling. Through the power of the Holy Spirit and the wisdom of others, I realized that it was not *doing* laundry that was most important to my wife, but that she had a partner to share life with.

The self-esteem part of it was *huge* for me (Mary). As long as I can remember I have been an overachiever. Early on in high school, I set my goals on being the top student in my class. I not only wanted to get all *A*s, but I wanted to get higher *A*s than any of my smart friends. I wanted to be Valedictorian of my class. It wasn't my parents or my friends that told me to do that; I pushed myself to do that—and to be head cheerleader and vice president of student council.

That carried over into other parts of my life when I graduated high school and went on to college. I wanted to support myself while I went to college, and so I worked a few jobs while I took a full load of classes, graduating in four years with a bachelor of science in Communicative Disorders and a teaching credential as well. I didn't know anyone else in speech who had done that, but it didn't matter to me. I thrived on stress and being told that something couldn't be done.

My favorite verse was Philippians 4:13, which told me that I could do ALL things through Christ who gave me strength. I certainly needed Christ and depended on Him to get me through college and graduate school. So it was not a *huge* change for me to be overloaded when I found myself handling things alone at home and with our family and businesses. In fact, I was pretty proud of myself that I could do it all. I loved it when a friend would say to me, "Mary, I don't know how you do it all" or "You pack more into a day than most of us do in a week." That was awesome! I loved hearing statements like that, and they only fueled the fire.

Obsessiveness

"Wait a minute, Craig. I'll give you the self-esteem piece of this four-part puzzle, but I'm not sure what you were talking about with the denial part; and I *know* I'm not obsessive." I understand. (I'll pause for a moment so you can text someone at the office. Are you back?) That's what I'm talking about. I could be reading a book, and all the while I was seeing how it would come across in a leadership lesson I could teach to my team. To put it bluntly, I was always thinking about work. While I was driving, while I was in bed, while I was watching television, my mind was constantly engaged and preoccupied with work. I ran on hyper-adrenaline with a broken gauge that monitored my ability to relax.

Obsessiveness to me (Mary) looked a little different. I had to have things done a certain way. The towels had to be folded just right, the dishwasher loaded correctly, the checkbook balanced in a certain program, the kids going out the door in ironed clothes every day . . . and the list went on and on. I couldn't ask someone else to help me, because they could potentially do it wrong, and then I might have to redo it.

It was difficult for me to turn cooking over to Craig one night a week, not because I didn't need help or want help, but because he would do it wrong. What if he didn't serve a salad with the pizza? Asking the kids to help took a lot of energy, because they would have to be trained to do it right, checked on repeatedly and then I'd have to redo their work when it was not good enough. Even Craig didn't have the same "standards" that I did, and it amazed me that he could sit and watch a sports game when, heaven forbid, there were dirty dishes in the sink. To make matters worse, he would ask me to come sit with him and watch too! Sit? Impossible until the dishes were done. I literally felt guilty sitting down with the dishes undone. It was as if they were screaming at me.

Blame

After I (Craig) realized my workaholism was hurting myself and my family, I moved to the next phase: blame. I found myself blaming my work culture for my hurried pace and out-of-balance living. It's easier to blame others than take responsibility for yourself. Yes, the culture you work in may be unhealthy. Yes, the boss you work for may give you more work than you can handle. Even if both of these things are true, and you are feeling the result of it, you can't blame them. Yes, I believe that bosses, leaders and cultures that have an unhealthy atmosphere and pace need to take responsibility for their workplace environment. But that's different than your blaming them for your overwork. There *are* cultures that promote more hectic than healthy atmospheres. When you blame your boss or work environment for your inability to find life balance, you are simply delaying your own path to health.

The same was true for me (Mary) at home. I blamed Craig for not helping out enough around the house. While that was a piece of it, it certainly wasn't the whole pie. I had to learn to let things go around the house and learn how to relax. I had to figure out how to let the kids, Craig and staff members help me. To be honest, I still struggle with this today. It seems easier for me to do things myself than to let others help me. But I find that it is often because I have unrealistic standards. The problem is, I also have unrealistic time frames. And I have to deal with the reality of that and see the whole picture in light of my season of life. What is the most important thing right now? What are my priorities? Is my to-do list matching my priorities?

The simple truth is, if you're a fast-paced, type A, firstborn (or only) in birth order, and you end up working at a place that mirrors your personality, it's a disaster waiting to happen. You will get burned out. You won't find balance, and it will get bitter before it gets better. It's important to think ahead to where you want to be so you can plan for health now. Stubbornness, rigidity, self-centeredness and a controlling personality round out the list of characteristics of a workaholic. Too stubborn to change, too rigid to get help, too self-centered to admit the problem and too controlling to let others help. I'm not citing a survey or clinical study, just giving a testimony. It's important to think ahead to where you want to be so that you can plan for health now.

I Am NOT Stressed! I'm NOT! I'm NOT! I'm NOT!

Workaholism and stress go together like Tom and Jerry of animal cartoon fame. Where you see one, you see the other. While filming a wakeboard curriculum series for elementary students in Florida a few years ago, I learned a few things about boats, the wake they create and how talented gold-medal wakeboarders are. When we arrived at the location, the boat was being prepped and the crew was setting up. I had to review a few things, so I went to sit in the boat and look at my notes. As I was getting into the boat, I noticed a few large rubber bags sitting on the floor of the boat. I thought this would be a good time to put my foot in my mouth, so I said, "Do you want me to take these bags out of the boat before we start?" The collective response from the crew and our gold-medal wakeboard friends were, "No, we need to fill them with water." I could not for the life of me figure out why someone would want to put water *in* the boat. I was later told that the water bags were necessary so the boat would sit lower in the water. When the boat sits lower in the water, it displaces more water and creates more waves behind the boat for the wakeboarder.

Like a wakeboarder's boat, workaholics can leave a large wake as they speed through the waters of life. The additional bags on the floor are filled with appointments, new ideas, brainstorming sessions and business lunches that allow their boat to sink lower, displace more water and create a bigger wake for those they pull behind. The wake means those being pulled behind need a strong sense of balance to simply stay on top of the water.

I have driven too many "boats" to count and have pulled too many people into the wake of what I was creating, never turning around to see what I was leaving behind me. Pulling friends and loved ones into your wake of stress happens too often in churches and businesses today. If you are a boat driver, then you may want to take care to drive slowly and watch the aggressive turns you make. They only produce more wake and more stress for those you are pulling behind.

Now, I don't believe all stress is bad. Some stress is actually good for us. It's true. The word "eustress" is defined as "stress that is deemed healthful or giving one the feeling of fulfillment."[4] You may be thinking the same thing I was thinking when I read that definition, and that was, "Are you serious?" I thought all stress was bad for you. Well, apparently there is some stress that's good for you. The kind of stress that does our body good is the kind of stress that *ends*!

As it turns out, *eustress,* or the good kind of stress, is the kind that is intermittent and occasional. It's not prolonged; it comes to an end. Good stress is positive only because it's not continual. If you go to the gym, run, jog or do some type of workout, you know the value of stop. You only work out for a short period of time. After your workout, you allow for adequate rest and recovery time so your muscles can heal and get stronger. In the gym, short-term stress followed by a time of rest equals a pathway to health. On the job, short-term stress followed by a time of rest equals a pathway to health as well.

However, when we allow stress to become *chronic* and *continual,* we get into trouble. Prolonged stress without rest and recovery will put us into a state of distress. In fact, if you repeatedly overwork a certain part of your body at the gym, with no time for rest, you can develop stress fractures in the bones of your arms or legs. When I played baseball in college, I developed a stress fracture in the elbow of my throwing arm. As the doctor reviewed the X-rays, he told me the tiny fractures in my elbow were a result of repetitive motion and overuse. He went on to tell me that the only remedy was to take some time off and allow my arm to heal.

Chronic and continual stress can lead to more than simple stress fractures in your bones; it can lead to death. The Japanese have a word for this: "*Karoshi,* meaning sudden death from overwork. . . . The first case of *karoshi* was initially called occupational sudden death."[5] Stress may start in your mind, but it ends up in your body through insomnia, worry, anxiety and heart disease, to name a few.

That's bad news for the boat *driver.* But what about those you are pulling behind? Usually, when I'm stressed, there are three words that can describe me: "inflexible," "impatient" and "irritable." All three of these words affect not only me, but also those around me.

When the book of Exodus was written, there were no smart phones, no computers, no Xboxes, no iPads or movie theaters, no baseball practice, no football practice, no soccer or basketball practice, no television. Life had less stuff, less choice, less clutter. I'm not saying they had less stress, but I will say that it was a different stress. Back when Moses was roaming around, there's no doubt life was tough, but their pace of life was much different from ours. Modern society hasn't helped us reduce our stress; rather, it has compounded it. Our culture can contribute to our chaos, but I'm not sure it can be blamed for it. Blaming today's fast-paced culture of fast food and smart phones for our increasing tendencies to overwork is like blaming 7-Eleven for Slurpees. Remember, wherever you go, there *you* are. First we have to treat the *you* and the *me.*

How can you reduce the stress in your life? How can you reduce the stress in the lives of others who do life with you? How can you create less wake behind you as you move through the waters of life? Perhaps having a proper perspective is a healthy first step. I'm pretty sure we weren't designed to do it all. God was doing fine before us. He is doing fine with us. And He will be doing fine when we are gone. We shouldn't try to tackle every opportunity that comes our way.

Like Mary, I would occasionally put a biblical spin on my overwork and say, "I can do everything through Christ who strengthens me" (Phil. 4:13, *GOD'S WORD*). I don't think Paul's words mean that we do everything, but that in everything we do, Christ gives us strength.

We don't need to do everything. Psalm 127:2 is a great reminder for us: "It is useless for you to work so hard from early morning until late at night, anxiously working for food to eat; for God gives rest to his loved ones."

7

OPEN UP

Courage is what it takes to stand up and speak;
courage is also what it takes to sit down and listen.

WINSTON CHURCHILL

How to Fake It

I was sitting in one of the pews of my kids' school assembly five years ago, answering emails on my phone while waiting for the principal to dismiss all of us dads to go into our children's classes. You see, it was Dad's Day at the school. We had already started off the morning by having pancakes with our kids out on the picnic tables. Then the kids filed off to their classes and the dads went to the chapel for a few announcements and to hear from the principal.

The school administration proceeded to hand out awards at the end of the program to parents who had volunteered for various things. I would mentally check out of these types of announcements due to the fact that I will never win a parent award. As you know by now, I am too busy doing other things. The last award they handed out was given to "The Dad of the Year." Just before the announcement, a ministry friend of mine leaned over to me; and while still reading emails on his phone, he said, "We'll never have to worry about getting that award." I nodded and smiled in agreement.

The next words out of the principal's mouth stunned me. It felt like I was in a dream and everything around me was happening in slow motion. I heard her say, "The Dad of the Year is Craig Jutila." My jaw dropped; my friend's jaw dropped. I literally couldn't move. In fact, I was afraid to get up. I hadn't been paying attention to the announcements or the awards. I didn't want to stand up in case the announcement was for something else, like parking my car in the wrong spot or leaving my lights on. The principal knew where I was sitting. She was looking directly at me as she gestured for me to come up to the stage.

I stood up on wobbly legs and inched down the center aisle, still wondering if this was a dream, a bad joke or if I had indeed left my car's headlights on. Somehow I made my way to the stage and received my award.

When the assembly concluded, I got a few high fives and handshakes from other parents and made my way to Cameron's and Alec's classrooms. After the festivities concluded, I went out to my car and sat there in silence for about 30 minutes.

I had just been selected Dad of the Year. My name would be forever etched in a plaque on the wall at my kids' school, yet my life was falling apart. I was most likely a few months away from divorce. I didn't like being home, Mary didn't like living with me. We fought too much, and my priorities were a joke. I had become a plastic person who could fake a certain life in front of others and live a different one at home; and what's worse, I was getting pretty good at it.

I can remember my dad's words as I played baseball growing up. He would always tell me to never believe your own press. At a young age, I didn't really know what he was talking about. As I got older, it made sense. While in high school, we were playing a game in the state of Washington for the Western United States Regional Colt League Championship and a chance to advance to the Colt League World Series. We won our first game of the series, followed by an article written about me, as I went four for four that game, with three runs batted in. I bought the paper, read and believed my own press and thought to myself, *This guy is good.*

My coach and my dad were both telling me something different. They kept telling me to forget that game, it was in the past, and to not believe my own press. Dad reminded me that my defense needed work. I wanted to hand him the article and ask him if he knew who he was talking to.

The next game came and went. The third game came and lingered. We were in the late innings of a close game. There were two outs and runners on first and third. I was playing third base at the time. The batter hit a routine ground ball my way. I could have easily moved to my right to get in the proper position to field the ball. Instead I decided to backhand it. *Routine play,* I thought to myself. In the casualness of the moment and the arrogance of my mind, I didn't field the ball cleanly, and it rolled off the heel of my glove and about 10 feet behind me where the dirt of the infield met the grass. The runner from third scored, and I was charged with an error.

The next day in the paper, there was a picture of me dropping the ball—a half-page picture of me on the front page of the sports section with the caption, "Run scores as Jutila boots ball." My dad's words resonated with me in that moment: "You are never as good as your greatest accomplishment, and you are never as bad as your worst failure." I didn't buy that newspaper, but my dad did. He bought it as a reminder for me. After talking to me about the error, he threw the paper away and encouraged me to do the same with the first one. I believe that's what our heavenly Father would do if He sat down next to you or me: "Rest in the fact that you are simply My son, and nothing can change that."

There I sat in the car, starting to believe my own press again, unaware that pride was creeping in. I couldn't wait to tell Mary that I was Dad of the Year at Alec and Cameron's school. I was even thinking, *That will show her. She has been wrong this whole time. I am a good father. She is the one with high expectations. I am a good husband.*

As it turns out, the Dad of the Year award wasn't actually saying that they thought I was a great dad to my kids, but a great dad to the school. That year, I had spoken a few times to their staff and given them all a copy of a book I wrote called *Leadership Essentials*. Apparently, this award was in recognition of my contribution to the time, energy and support I had given the staff of the school, not in recognition of the quality of my fatherhood with my children.

You may be reading this section and saying, "My wife (or my husband) is constantly riding me about my schedule. She just doesn't understand my job. Her expectations are too high." My own experience tells me that a spouse usually makes a pretty accurate assessment. We all need to listen to our spouse. They may not *always* be right, but I am almost certain that your spouse will have a better success rate on the truth about you than what your press tells you, or your staff or team, or your next-door neighbor. Perhaps it's time to open up and get real about your current situation.

Guys Don't Talk in the Bathroom

Why don't guys talk with each other in the bathroom? Because we're not supposed to. That's the simple answer. It's weird. It's wrong. It's a guy thing. Also, guys do not go with other guys to the bathroom for the same reasons.

Gals are different. I (Craig) have observed, on a number of occasions, a *group* of women heading for the lavatory. When Mary and I are out to dinner with other couples, I've witnessed that frequently one of the wives will say, "I'm going to the ladies room. Does anyone else want to go?" Then all of the ladies proceed to walk off together.

Mary tells me that not only do women talk in the bathroom, but it is possible to make new friends anytime they go in there. I can't explain it and it doesn't make sense to me. (And you wonder why husbands and wives have a hard time communicating.)

Guys usually communicate on the surface with each other, and never in the bathroom. I was out playing golf with a couple of good friends of mine, Ron and Rudy. Depending on the pace of play, a round of golf can last between four and five hours, and maybe another hour for lunch. A conservative guess is that I can spend five hours playing golf with my friends riding next to me and eat lunch with them only to drive home and have Mary ask me, "How's Ron and Rudy?" to which I reply, "I don't know."

Then the conversation goes something like this. "I thought you were playing golf with them today."

"Yes, we played Tijeras Creek today."

"And you don't know how they are doing?"

"How would *I* know how they are doing?"

"You mean to tell me that you were with Ron and Rudy for five hours today, playing the same golf course, riding next to each other in the same cart and eating lunch at the same table, and you honestly don't know how they are doing?"

"Well, I know Ron and Rudy each shot 86 and they are both having trouble with their short game. Oh, and Rudy has a new putter."

If I (Mary) had five hours to spend with a close friend, I would return home knowing what was going on with her husband, her daughter's teacher, her son's basketball team, a new recipe she had tried that week, where they were going to vacation, as well as when we would get together again. And she would know all about what was going on in my life. If we weren't going to *talk*, then why in the world get together? To me, that would be a *complete* waste of time. Before I understood that this non-talking thing was seemingly universal, I seriously wondered if Craig had even *seen* his friends that day.

You can see the dilemma, not only for our relationship as guys with other guys, but how God wired men and women so differently. I don't understand. I'm sorry, *we* (guys) don't understand how you gals can make friends with a stranger in the bathroom. And not only make friends but find out how many kids they have, the age of those children, where they work, their husband's names and where they were born, where they shop and what toothpaste they use, all in five minutes. This equally blows a guy's mind.

Guys not only don't talk in the bathroom, but they also rarely open up and share their weaknesses with others when the situation has been carefully orchestrated to provide an environment to do so. We like to test the waters before revealing too much. We need to spend some time surveying the group or the person to see if they/he can be trusted. Once we have determined that the person or environment is safe, it usually comes down to a couple of things. We are afraid to appear weak, and we certainly don't want others to know that we don't have it all together. The short sentence is that we are afraid and arrogant.

My experience has been that most guys who end up in counseling have been begged, prodded, pleaded, dragged or in some way leveraged by their wives. I have met people, around the country, who will not go to counseling because they are afraid they will be seen. I have already given my testimony to that fact. Some guys will go so far as to drop their wife off at counseling and then go run errands or sit in the car. Others refuse counseling because they counsel others and they think, *How on earth can someone else help me when I am doing the exact same thing to help others? Maybe I can implement some of the things I tell other couples to do and get my marriage back on line.*

Not too long ago, my family was at the beach. The kids were playing in the water, catching a few waves and having a good time. Mary and I were pleasantly situated in our beach chairs next to the cooler, lathered up with SPF 90 sunscreen and reading our Kindles. We were right next to one of the lifeguard stations that are situated about a hundred yards apart from each other. It wasn't a particularly crowded day on the beach, and the waves were unusually flat. Both Mary and I noticed the lifeguard come out to the front of his tower with a pair of binoculars. After a brief look and assessment, he decided to walk to the water's edge for a closer look. All seemed to be pretty calm to us, but to the watchful eye of a trained lifeguard there was something amiss.

Suddenly, he was yelling out to one of the guys swimming in the ocean. He was telling him to swim parallel to the beach. The swimmer was tired and could not get out of a developing rip tide. A rip tide—actually it's a rip current—is a powerful and narrow current of water that runs perpendicular to the beach and out to the ocean. You can get a feeling for a rip current by standing in knee deep ocean water along the beach while the waves ebb and flow. As the water flattens out and runs up onto the beach you may feel off balance because the force is pushing you up the beach. When the water starts to recede, you may feel like you are being pulled out into the ocean. That's the feeling of a rip current, but with one exception. When you are caught in a rip current, your feet are not firmly planted on the sand; instead you are swimming on top of the water with absolutely nothing to stabilize you. Occasionally, a tired swimmer can get caught in a rip current and not survive its effects.

The situation we were watching unfold that day led to drastic measures. The rip current was pulling the swimmer farther and farther into the ocean. The swimmer knew what to do to escape the current, but he was simply overwhelmed by his situation. Fatigue had set in, and his calmness was quickly giving way to panic and disorientation. However, not once did the lifeguard say, "You can do it! Just believe. I have seen you get out of this situation before." No. The lifeguard ran into the water, swam out and rescued the distressed swimmer. The swimmer had pulled others out of such a current before. Yet, now he needed help, which the lifeguard provided. That's what lifeguards do. They help, they rescue, they save, and sometimes they restore life in what could be a devastating end.

Occasionally, we get caught in relational rip currents. Sometimes we get caught in the rip current of life. You may know how to get out of life's rip current. You may have read several books on rip currents, attended a rip current class, taken a rip current seminar. Hey, you may have written a book titled *How to Get Out of a Spiritual Rip Current*. But occasionally, fatigue sets in; calmness turns to panic in our relationships. We get disoriented and in need of rescue.

I'm sure the gentleman in the water was grateful for the helping hand that day. I don't think he was going to say, "Hey, why did you pull me out of that rip current back there? I wrote a book on rip currents and did a 12-part series on them. What on earth were you thinking? Most of the people on this beach have read that book or heard that series, and now you jump in and help me. How embarrassing is that?"

As life gets more difficult and painful, you will be more likely to leave your feelings of fear and pride in order to have a deeper conversation that will help you. But honestly, it's easier said than done. It was for me.

Courageous Words

I used several strategies when I didn't want to open up and talk about the hidden hurts or hang-ups in my life. The most basic and most used tactic was to ignore and avoid. You can easily accomplish this through text and email messages. When someone asked me in a text or email how I was doing, I would usually give the standard "I'm okay, and you?" response. This would satisfy those who were most likely asking out of obligation anyway. The other people, who genuinely cared for me and were asking out of kindness, love and concern, were met with the sound of digital silence. In short, I would simply not respond. I would let the text or email sit in digital captivity until they forgot they had sent it. Occasionally, I would respond with a question or comment to divert the conversation entirely. I got pretty good at it.

Opening up your life and telling others something other than the standard answer to the question "How are you?" isn't easy, but it is necessary to connect on a deeper level relationally. To open up and be authentic, to share your life with a close inner circle of friends, is no doubt difficult. It was for Mary and me. If you have been burned by what you have shared with others, Satan will do what he can to leverage that pain in his unhealthy favor. "Hold it in," he will whisper. "Don't share your difficulty with someone else. They will burn you like the last person did." Lies, lies and more lies. James 5:16 is a far cry from holding it in. This verse tells us, "Confess your sins to each other and pray for each other so that you may be healed. The earnest prayer of a righteous person has great power and wonderful results" (Jas. 5:16).

It's fairly easy to talk about the weather, sports or today's headlines; but it's incredibly difficult to say to someone, "Uh . . . yeah, ummm, I have a problem with lying," or "I am extremely arrogant and self-centered." It's always a possibility that if we open up and share our stuff, the other person might say or think, "Geez, you are really messed up. I can't believe how dysfunctional you are." I have never had anyone say that to me. Sometimes I have seen it in their eyes and body language. But just remember that the secrets you are hiding are most likely equal in number to the secrets of the person sitting next to you. So, if we could all say a collective, "I'll share my stuff if you share your stuff," life would be so much richer. Wouldn't it?

When you reveal the junk about your life to others, there is a substantial risk involved. The person may disconnect from you. That's rejection. He or she may tell others about your situation. That's painful. He or she may lecture you. That's humiliating. You have read the first section in this book about when I had to *pay* someone to listen to me. I say that with a smile and tongue in cheek, but the fact is, I was afraid. I was afraid I would lose friends. I was afraid I would appear weak. I was afraid people would talk about me. I didn't want to risk letting others know I didn't have it all together. I'm a pastor; I'm supposed to have it all together. Courage, that's what was lacking. Call it what you will—an inability to open up or an aversion to sharing deeply—but the bottom line was *fear*.

Jesus promises us something different—something substantial. Hebrews 4:15-16 tells us, "This High Priest of ours understands our weaknesses, for he faced all of the same temptations we do, yet he did not sin. So let us come boldly to the throne of our gracious God. There, we will receive His mercy, and we will find grace to help us when we need it." "Understanding," "mercy," "grace." What great words! What a great picture.

What if we could all open up and say, "No matter what you tell me, I will not judge, blame or condemn you." What if we could exhibit that perfect love that casts out fear so that others would feel comfortable opening up?

I didn't have courageous words until I was knee-deep in fear. I still struggle with letting people know who I really am. The fear of rejection runs deep. I always felt I needed to be the best pastor, leader, parent or spouse anyone had ever seen. I needed to be an example, and if I shared my life openly and honestly with others, they would see that I didn't have it all together.

I was supposed to be counseling people who needed my help, yet I wouldn't go to counseling myself. I would tell people they needed to be better parents, but I was failing miserably in that area. I would talk about the importance of date nights with one's spouse, but I wasn't planning them for my wife. I would tell people to forgive their past hurts, yet I was holding on to bitterness in my life. That kind of expectation without authenticity was causing a dilemma in my soul. After years of faking it, my soul had become numb. It became easier to fake spirituality than take care of my own soul.

The reminder here for all of us is found in Philippians: "You must be even more careful to put into action God's saving work in your lives, obeying God with deep reverence and fear. For God is working in you, giving you the desire to obey Him and the power to do what pleases Him" (Phil. 2:12-13). Yes, God is working in our lives. He is giving us the power. However, I don't think God will do what we won't do. Look specifically at the words Paul penned in verse 12: "Put into action God's saving work in your lives."

We want so desperately to risk with others, to say, "I know I am supposed to be the example here, but I don't have it all together. In fact, I don't even have it half together. My marriage is in survival mode; my kids are out of control. I don't have any close friends and I struggle with sin that's not even mentioned in the Bible. Can someone please help me?"

There is a reason the Bible says to "confess your sins to one another, and pray for one another." The reason is "so that you may be healed" (Jas. 5:16, *NASB*). It's easy to understand the prayer part, but what about the confession part? According to the apostle James, it's equally as important as praying for one another. James is saying, "Take a risk; be candid. Be authentic with what you say and how you live your life." There is no other way to be spiritually healthy.

The difficulty with being authentic is that the people with whom we are being authentic may not be reciprocal in their authenticity. Have you ever fallen victim to that? Me too. What if you back up your emotional truck and only dump half of it, and as you take a breath to get a response, the words "I'll definitely be praying for you" get released in your direction. Well, that's where the courage comes in; the courage to be real and genuine isn't for the faint of heart, but for the resilient. To share your previous pain and hurt and say what is really going on inside of you is not the easiest thing to do. Yet James gives us a mandate to do it.

I am not saying jump in and speak your mind like water coming out of a fire hydrant. In fact, some of us need to hold our tongues on occasion. But words shared authentically, from a perspective of "I don't have it all together," and seasoned with humility, grace and love can make a huge difference in others' lives and in your own life. But you must be courageous.

After the death of Moses, the Lord spoke to Joshua, letting him know that he was going to lead God's people across the Jordan River and into the land of Canaan (see Josh. 1). This was no easy task. The role of leading, with that many people following, called for an incredibly high level of skill, monumental faith and extraordinary courage. Joshua wasn't told to lead a small group across a stream; he was told to lead a nation across a river! He was appointed to follow Moses who, by the way, happened to be a great leader. As the Lord spoke to Joshua, He laid out the plan for his future—a daunting future, to say the least. As God continued to speak with Joshua, there was a recurring theme that is recorded throughout the first nine verses of Joshua, specifically in verses 6, 7 and 9.

Verse 6 says, "Be strong and courageous." Verse 7 says, "Be strong and *very* courageous." Verse 9 says, "I *command* you—be strong and courageous!" (emphasis added). The progression moves from a prompt to a push to a proclamation. It seems to me that courage is more of a duty and a responsibility than a point to ponder. We must be courageous, because He is with us!

God told Joshua to "be strong and courageous." He wanted Joshua to be determined and confident as he led God's people, something every leader needs in order to be effective. In verse 7, the Lord repeats the encouragement to be strong and courageous but adds the word "very." The word "very" can mean abundantly, greatly or exceedingly. It's the same word that's used in Genesis 7:18: "The waters rose and increased *greatly* on the earth" (*NIV*, emphasis added). This should give us a vivid word picture of how passionately God was communicating to Joshua. He wanted Joshua to understand that with his new role would come risk, danger and difficulty; so He needed Joshua to be abundantly courageous, greatly courageous, exceedingly courageous!

After nudging Joshua to be courageous, God jumped to a command: "I *command* you, be strong and courageous!" Why the energy, God? Because whether we like it or not, whether we convey it or not, there was fear in Joshua, and that's a good thing, because you can't have courage without fear.

If we're honest about it, there is fear in each one of us too. I don't think any of us is being asked to do what Joshua did in facing insurmountable odds to lead a large group of people to a place they hadn't been before, with danger at almost every turn. But if the truth be told, perhaps you would rather be in Joshua's shoes than sitting in front of a friend or small group about to reveal your inner secrets. "Bring on the crowd!" you may feel like shouting. It's easier for some of us to lead and get lost in a crowd than to be authentic and vulnerable in front of a few close friends. But the duty and responsibility are the same. Be strong and *very* courageous! Let us face that fear head-on, with courageous words, because God is with us!

While his job was being threatened by an aggressive attorney general in the movie *The Kingdom*, FBI Director James Grace, played by actor Richard Jenkins, speaks a powerful and courageous truth when he says, "You know, Westmoreland made all of us officers write our own obituaries during Tet . . . and once we clued into the fact that life is finite, the thought of losing it didn't scare us anymore. The end comes no matter what, the only thing that matters is how do you wanna go out, on your feet or on your knees?"[1]

The end does eventually come for all of us, and I would prefer to go out risking it all standing on a rock of courage than the sand of fear.

8

PAUSE OFTEN

Observe the Sabbath day by keeping it holy, as the Lord your God has commanded you. Six days a week are set apart for your daily duties and regular work, but the seventh day is a day of rest dedicated to the Lord your God.

DEUTERONOMY 5:12-14

Sabbath Shmabbath

The word "Sabbath" means to cease or rest. It is a weekly pause to refresh from work. The Sabbath was created and implemented by God Himself at the end of His six days of the creation of the world. We are told in Genesis 1:31, "God saw all that he had made, and it was very good," and in Genesis 2:2, "By the seventh day God had finished the work he had been doing; so on the seventh day he rested from all his work" (*NIV*). God ceased from His work because He saw that it was good *and* He was finished.

Our problem is that we are rarely satisfied with "good," and we have a tendency to think that nothing is ever "finished." The Sabbath is a time to not only rest our bodies but also our hearts and minds. Most times, even though my body is relaxing, my mind is busy creating more things for my body to do. No doubt that's a symptom of a deeper underlying problem. I'm feeling guilty that I am not working, anxious because I would rather be working or busy writing things down to do when I start working again tomorrow.

For the most part, we live in a culture that tells us our value comes largely from what we do and how well we do it. As a result, many of us are driven to work harder, stay longer, and build bigger and better churches, companies and careers. If you take a closer look at the last two letters of each of those words you will find they end in "ER," which is where you'll end up if you subscribe to that sort of thinking. Not only was I a subscriber, but I was also a publisher of this line of thought. *Bigger, bigger, bigger; more, more, more.* Jesus never practiced the bigger is better or the more is better approach. In fact He said, "I have a lot more to tell you, but that would be too much for you now" (John 16:12, *GOD'S WORD*).

While speaking at a conference in Atlanta, Georgia, I excused myself between sessions. I felt sick to my stomach, so I headed for the men's room. While leaning forward over the sink with my head down, I began to cough up blood. *What should I do?* Yep, let's head back out there and teach another session like nothing is wrong.

When I returned home, I went to our doctor, who suggested I stop burning the candle at both ends. If you don't, you will run out of wax twice as fast. Of course, I didn't take the advice. I decided to ignore words like "rest," "refill," "replenish" and "refresh," not to mention the advice of my doctor. Sure, I took a few days off, but as soon as I started to feel better, I was right back out there chasing the wind. I didn't take the Sabbath command literally. I mean, it's in the Old Testament, right? *Sabbath, Shmabbath.*

Apparently, God takes it a bit more seriously. As He spoke instructions to Moses, He said, "Yes, keep the Sabbath day, for it is holy. Anyone who desecrates it must die; anyone who works on that day will be cut off from the community. Work six days only, but the seventh day must be a day of total rest. I repeat: Because the LORD considers it a holy day, anyone who works on the Sabbath must be put to death" (Exod. 31:14-15). I would say that's taking it pretty seriously. If you didn't observe it, if you didn't practice it, if you didn't take the Sabbath seriously, you would be put to death. How many of us would take a closer look at the Sabbath command if not keeping it meant the death penalty? God set up the Sabbath after Creation for the purpose of rest. He still takes it seriously. He instituted and observed the Sabbath, and so should we.

My (Mary's) first experience with the Sabbath was when I was a student at Loma Linda University in Southern California. At registration, I received a school calendar and noticed there was something on the calendar that was never on a calendar I had owned before: sunset time on Friday and Saturday nights. Loma Linda University is an Adventist University, and the school calendar lists the times when the Sabbath starts and when it ends. On Fridays, there were no classes after noon, because professors and students needed that time to prepare for the Sabbath. My Adventist friends told me that their moms would shop, bake and prepare food for that evening and the following day. The kids had chores they needed to complete to get the house clean and ready for Sabbath. Their best clothes were ironed and ready for the following day. Some even removed magazines and books from their coffee tables and turned the television off. "Sabbath is about atmosphere, a radical change of pace, about finding space for God; about making time for special communion with Him."[1]

I was amazed at the routines my friends practiced on Friday nights, which included a meal and worship, as well as a lesson. On Saturday morning, they attended church and ate lunch together, usually potluck style with everyone bringing a dish from home to share after the service. There was so much community and fellowship happening among the people. On the Sabbath, the stores were closed, and you weren't even supposed to study or do schoolwork until sundown on Saturday. I saw value placed not only *on* the Sabbath rest, but also *in* the Sabbath rest. It showed me that I needed a day of rest, but I had no time built into my schedule for it. It made me realize why God had made it a law in the Old Testament. If He hadn't, if it had been optional, I'm sure no one would have chosen to observe it.

On the Sabbath day, we're called to not only stop working but also to empty ourselves of our guilt to get other things done. It's less about doing and more about being. Now, how many of us really use our Sabbath for that? Most of us believe the word "Sabbath" is Hebrew for errands. I (Craig) don't think we should look at our modern Sabbath as a day off. Who really has a day off? The Sabbath was for the stopping of work, not for running errands, right? I would call errands work. They aren't the work or the job you get a paycheck from, but they are work. Shouldn't we, then, have two days off from the job we get paid to do? One for the Sabbath and one for errands and getting all the other things done we can't get done while we are at work?

If you look further into Sabbath, you will find out there is more to it than just a day of rest. If we are going to take Sabbath seriously, then why not jump in all the way? Along with the weekly day of rest, there was also a Sabbatical year. Yes, *a year*. One definition says that Sabbath is "a season or day of rest."[2]

According to Leviticus 25, when God was talking to Moses, He gave him these instructions: "For six years you may plant your fields and prune your vineyards and harvest your crops, but during the seventh year the land will enjoy a Sabbath year of rest to the LORD. Do not plant your crops or prune your vineyards during that entire year" (Lev. 25:3-4). These verses are the basis for modern culture's sabbatical, usually observed by college and university professors, and occasionally by pastors from various denominations. The modern sabbatical usually involves time off to write a book or conduct research for a project or increase one's knowledge and leadership by reading a select set of books or articles. In essence, a modern sabbatical has changed from the act of ceasing to the act of increasing through some sort of activity. I'm not sure that was its original intention.

I was talking to a friend about his summer, specifically about how he spent nine weeks of it. What he told me caught me off guard and prompted several questions regarding his company, his co-workers and their culture. Dan works for a very large and successful Fortune 100 company. Out of that top 100, his company, Intel, appears in the top five of Fortune 500's best companies to work for.

Dan has worked for Intel for seven years. He told me some of the things that make this such a great place to work. There was one specific benefit that jumped out to me. After you have worked at Intel for seven years, you get a nine-week sabbatical to do, uh . . . nothing. Now that's a sabbatical!

His company implements cross-training throughout their departments so that when your paid time off begins, your co-workers cover your particular role and responsibilities within the organization. Dan had just enjoyed nine weeks away from work with his family—traveling, visiting and connecting with friends and family during this extended vacation period.

It appears that more and more companies are discovering the importance of balancing work life and personal life. *Forbes* magazine said, "We find each year that work-life balance is a key factor in determining employee happiness. . . . Employees want to know that they can balance their career with their family and personal life. Often this reigns over things like salary."[3] After my conversation with Dan, I can confirm this to be true. How do you put a price tag on nine weeks paid time off with your family?

In a world where we are in desperate need of pause and rest, companies like Intel are practicing the biblical concept of the sabbatical year by giving their staff a much-needed pause to rest, refill, replenish and refresh their lives. What would happen to a person's soul, emotional health, mental state and overall attitude if companies and churches started to implement sabbaticals for their staff?

I'll Be There in a Minute

In chapter 5, we walked through the narrative of a very busy ministry day with Jesus and His disciples. People were coming and going so constantly that Jesus and the disciples didn't even have time to eat. They left by boat for a quieter spot, but the crowd followed, and the people were waiting on the other side when the boat reached the shore. Thousands gathered, and as the day drew to a close, the disciples were without food for the people. Jesus performed a miracle with a little boy's lunch of five loaves of bread and two fish. The narrative as the Gospel of Mark records it ends suddenly: "Immediately after this [the feeding of the 5,000], Jesus made his disciples get back into the boat and head out across the lake to Bethsaida, while he sent the people home" (Mark 6:45).

As I read through this verse in light of what Jesus and His disciples had just experienced, a word jumped out: "immediately," which is straightforward and to the point. Can you see the scene unfolding? There are thousands of people amazed at this miracle made from a little boy's lunch. The disciples, equally astounded, are trying to figure out what just happened and are hurling questions at Jesus or pondering amongst themselves about the miracle they have just witnessed. The crowd is still present. Some are sitting; others are walking and talking. Jesus is weary and tired from a long day in an earthly body. I can see Him herding the disciples toward the boat while fielding a constant stream of questions about what just happened. Jesus was intent on putting the disciples in the boat straightaway. "Guys, please get in the boat. I need you to just get in the boat. I will clean up; I will take care of the people. You go on now, and I will be there in a minute."

It's in verse 45 that another word catches my attention—the word "made." If you are a parent, you understand that word in a different way than those without children. Amen? The word "made" tells us there must have been at least one reluctant contributor amongst the disciples. If I had to venture a guess, I would say it was more than one. Nevertheless, Jesus "made" one or some of them get into that boat. Did Jesus raise His voice? Did He gently grab a shoulder? What was the expression on His face? I wish I had been there to see it. In that moment, with a crowd buzzing, the disciples questioning and the atmosphere humming, Jesus, with a high sense of urgency in His voice made 12 guys get into a boat they didn't want to get into and sent them away. This brings me to another point to ponder: Why send the staff away first?

If you have the pleasure and responsibility of leading a team of any size, you instinctively know the answer. Sometimes, the people you work with create more chaos than comfort; and at least in this moment, Jesus, although He was completely God, was also completely man. Perhaps He simply needed the questions, comments and concerns of the team to continue out on the lake while He remained on the shore. Why did He find it more suitable to stay and dismiss the thousands while the 12 rowed away? I don't know; but it's the way Jesus did it. We do know that after He said goodbye to the crowd, He went up into the hills by Himself to pray. Jesus moved from the chaos of the crowd to the quiet comfort; He went from a hectic place to a healthy pause.

What Time Is It?

A healthy pause requires deliberate action, at least for most of us. There's always so much to do. I know that my to-do list outpaces the amount of time I have available to accomplish it. Trying to manage time is like chasing the wind or trying to catch a cat by its tail. How do we accomplish any moments of pause when the culture we live in seems to be speeding up?

Sometimes I echo the words of Job when he said, "My life is speeding by, without a hope of happiness" (Job 9:25, CEV). I used to say, "Go with the flow," but in today's fast-paced and occasionally suffocating culture, that could mean that we may drown in the current.

One of the questions our kids ask frequently when we are traveling somewhere is about the time. "Dad, Dad . . . Mom, Mom, Mom, what time is it?" When I say, "The same time it was the last time you asked me," Alec will say, "Dad, it can't be the same time as the last time we asked. That's impossible. This isn't the Matrix." To which I reply, "Well, *technically* there was a time when it was the same time as the last time." It's true! Take a look at what happened when Joshua prayed for the sun and moon to stand still:

> On the day the LORD gave the Israelites victory over the Amorites, Joshua prayed to the LORD in front of all the people of Israel. He said, "Let the sun stand still over Gibeon, and the moon over the valley of Aijalon." So the sun and moon stood still until the Israelites had defeated their enemies. Is this event not recorded in The Book of Jashar? The sun stopped in the middle of the sky, and it did not set as on a normal day. The LORD fought for Israel that day. Never before or since has there been a day like that one, when the LORD answered such a request from a human being (Josh. 10:12-14).

This reference is the only place God's Word tells us He added more hours to someone's day. Wouldn't it be great to have the sun pause in the sky so we could have more time to work through a to-do list or prepare a report or plan an event? After reading Joshua 10:14, I don't think it's ever going to happen again. Life is going to move on with the same amount of time each and every day.

Another common "kid" question on a car trip is "Are we there yet?" Of course, the parental response is, "We will get there when we get there." But if you stop and think about these two questions—"What time is it?" and "Are we there yet?"—you realize they are brilliant questions. I should have been asking myself those questions for the last 20 years. How do you know if you have arrived at your destination if you don't know where you are going? If you don't know where you are going, how do you know where to spend your time? If you don't know where to spend your time, you end up spending it recklessly and without thought. We talk a lot about investing our money and spending our time, but it feels like we should reverse the thinking. Maybe we should invest our time and spend our money. It's just a thought.

Here's another way to look at it. What would happen if you won a contest and the prize was that each day at 6:00 AM, $86,400 was automatically deposited to your checking account? The only catch is that at the end of each day, any money you had not used would be removed from your account and completely zeroed out, all gone. If you think of time the way I think of time, then you probably say, "Oh well, I will get another $86,400 tomorrow." Apply that illustration to time instead of money. My mind automatically looks at time as a constant deposit to my life account; it's always there for me to make a withdrawal, so I don't value the amount in my account because it will always get replenished. I would like to get to a point where I view time as a commodity, or something that's limited or scarce. Maybe I wouldn't spend it so recklessly.

Today God has given each of us 86,400 seconds to use as we choose. That's 168 hours to spend or invest each week. The question is, "How are we managing our account?" Spending recklessly? Investing shrewdly? Each of us is responsible for how and where we invest. We can invest our time wisely or poorly. When you spend your money, you can always get more money. It may be hard to recapture your loss, but you can get more money. Time is different. When you spend your time, it's gone; you can never recapture the time you have spent. Doesn't it feel like time is more valuable than money? If that's the case, then we all make the same amount, and those who invest according to their life's season become the new rich. No longer is a big home on the hill and a great car in the driveway the measure of success. Success is measured by making the right time investments. That thinking may seem a bit upside down, but wouldn't you agree it's something to ponder?

There is a unique difficulty that plagues us during those 86,400 seconds. Various interruptions can and do rob us of our investment. A flat tire on the way to work, a hallway meeting at the office, people who are never on time, unexpected illness, traffic on the freeway, someone who wants more of your time or asks you to do more than you know you should or could, and the list goes on. It's called life, and these things are simply unavoidable. How do we deal with the tyranny of the urgent?

You may have spent most of your investment for today or this week. You may have budgeted for your week, but most of your investment is already accounted for; so when people come to make a withdrawal from the bank of YOU, and there isn't anything left, you give them a loan without even checking their references. If you had checked, you would have noticed they are in trouble with their investments as well. As the week draws to a close, you realize you are over budget and you have loaned out to others who have no intention of repaying. Now you are not only in default, but you are also emotionally, mentally and socially bankrupt. You have spent more than you have, and the debt collectors are knocking at your door. We pay for this with the only collateral we have left—stress in our body and strain in our relationships.

As a recovering workaholic, I would enjoy a few more hours in my day. But the Lord made the day and the evening to accomplish a natural ebb and flow of work and rest to help us remain in balance and keep a healthy pace. God even chose to rest a day when He was finished creating the world. I compounded working longer by not taking much-needed vacation time. A workaholic personality, when combined with a heart to make a difference, can sidetrack you a bit, depending on your current life season.

Someone recently asked me, "Craig, can you ever really walk away from an opportunity?" Today, I can honestly say, "Yes, I can. But it has taken five years to get to this point, and it still isn't easy." I have a tendency to look at all good opportunities as doors God is opening for me; and I walk right on through without ever making sure it's God who is opening them. What if it's the enemy? If our enemy can get us preoccupied with good, maybe we will miss better opportunities at another time. Just because the opportunity is good doesn't mean it's right for you in your particular life season. Just because a door is opening, it doesn't mean it is God who is unlocking it for you. Just because you *can* walk through an open door, it doesn't mean you should. The Bible says, "Teach us to make the most of our time, so that we may grow in wisdom" (Ps. 90:12).

SECTION 3

SETTING
PACE

9

PRACTICE
SOUL CARE

Guard your heart and guard your mind; nobody else is going to do it for you.
AUTHOR UNKNOWN

Guard Your Heart

We had a swim party at our house a while ago. Our friends Chris and Dawn were there with their three kids. Chris and Dawn have been in our small group for years. We have been friends longer than that. I performed their marriage ceremony; we played hockey together; and we have helped each other through the tough times as well as celebrated the good times. After the burgers and the watermelon had been devoured, it was time for the adults to hit the pool. Off came the shirts, and there it was—a tattoo on Chris's left arm. I'm not opposed to tattoos, but I was unaware that Chris had one. If you had asked me which of all my friends would be least likely to get a tattoo, I might even have said Chris. The words were tattooed around a heart and read, "Above all else, guard your heart, for it affects everything you do" (Prov. 4:23).

The word "guard" paints a picture of a watchful soldier looking out for an intruder, keeping someone or something safe from harm. The verse is telling us to keep our hearts safe. What is your heart exactly? The word "heart" in this verse is referring to our soul or our innermost being. It's the center of our thoughts, emotions, words and deeds. It says that out of the heart flows everything else. If we are not guarding our heart, the consequences can be disastrous. Jesus' words to a group of Pharisees remind us to be responsible for our soul care: "A tree is identified by its fruit. Make a tree good, and its fruit will be good. Make a tree bad, and its fruit will be bad. . . . How could evil men like you speak what is good and right? For whatever is in your heart determines what you say. A good person produces good words from a good heart, and an evil person produces evil words from an evil heart" (Matt. 12:33-35).

How do you protect your heart and thereby practice soul care? I (Mary) am not talking about doing routine "churchy" things like attending a worship service on the weekend or going to a midweek service or small group. Yes, these are great things, necessary things. But it's more than that. Guarding your heart doesn't involve only outward practices, but an inward process as well. I'm talking about something much more intimate, personal and private. To be honest, Craig and I had the spiritual routines down; but what we didn't have down were the private practices of soul care that no one on the outside could see. Some things needed to change—had to change—in order to practice and deepen our soul care. Of course, soul care takes something you don't have if you are living an overloaded, out-of-balance hectic life. Yes, it's that *T* word—time.

It's imperative that you spend time alone with God every day. This is not a "study time" to write a message for others to hear. It's not a daily task so that you can check something off your to-do list. Nor should it be done so that you can tell others you had your quiet time. It's a time when you stop to pause and meet God. You are open, honest, real and vulnerable with God, your Creator and your Abba Father. You share your worries, confess your sins, seek His wisdom and listen to His voice and what He has to say to you, just to *you*.

I (Craig) have found that when I spend more time in God's Word, I actually get more time back. It's ironic, because when I'm extremely busy, I usually find ways to skimp on certain things in my life. Quiet time can be one of them. I can remember going camping in the mountains in Southern California several years ago. We were playing a game with some of the youth who were on this trip. The rules of this particular game were to go hide and then sneak back into the camp undetected.

I remember sitting out in the forest that night, all by myself. At one point, when the clouds covered the moon, I could not see my hand in front of my face. I could hear the sound of those who had made it back into camp without getting caught, but I was stranded behind a rock and could not see to take another step. If I only had a flashlight, I could have easily found my way back into camp.

I ended up fumbling around in the darkness, tripping over rocks and bumping into obstacles until I made my way back. Once I got to my cabin, I found my flashlight and aimed it back up to where I had been hiding. Sure enough, there was a straight path back down into camp that would have taken me five minutes to walk. Instead it took me an hour to wander around the mountain before making it back. A poor use of time? Yep. Would a flashlight have helped? Yep.

God's Word gives us the same principle. The psalmist says, "Your word is a lamp for my feet and a light for my path" (Ps. 119:105). When you read God's Word, it exposes the right path for you to take and the route you should steer away from. Reading God's Word can and will illuminate your path and give you direction in a dark world.

While Craig and I were in a bookstore in London, we purchased a Moleskin book with lined pages that I like to use as a journal. It's a simple book, but what God has revealed to me on those pages has not only been life-changing, but also day-changing. Sometimes what I thought I was going to do that day changed after meeting with God that morning.

I can think of times when God brought a friend or family member to mind during my time with Him. I didn't know why or what was going on with that person, but with the Holy Spirit's urging, I felt that I needed to pray for that person and follow up to see what was happening in their life. When I did, I found they were going through a difficult time and were really in need of a friend to come alongside them.

I haven't always followed through on those leadings from the Holy Spirit, because I had my own agenda. I had my own list of things to accomplish on my calendar that sometimes left me feeling unfulfilled and unproductive. What if I had guarded my heart and listened to God's leading for that day instead of checking off things on my to-do list for the day? I wonder what God could have done through me?

Both Craig and I have learned that journaling is a huge part of guarding your heart. Journaling is a practice that has long been regarded by counselors as essential to emotional health. Journaling allows you to write down your thoughts, your feelings, your worries, your insights, so that you can understand them, organize them, learn from them and remember them. Journaling helps change the way you are thinking or feeling. Journaling is a valuable part of learning and growing and guarding your heart.

As we were writing this book, we took out all of our journals from the past few years and looked through them to see what we had learned, how God had spoken to us and what He had been teaching us. It was a reminder to both of us how important it is to journal so that we can have solid proof that God does answer our prayers and walk with us through difficult times. We can look back to see how and what we were feeling, and how God worked in our lives.

I (Mary) also write my prayer requests in my journal. This helps me to look back and see God's faithfulness and how He has taken care of our needs; and it encourages me to trust Him more. Praying is a vital part of soul care. If you think of reading God's Word as God's way to talk to you, then think of prayer as your talking to Him. You can tell Him anything in prayer. God wants you to give it all to Him. Dump it all at His feet and then don't worry about it anymore. I tend to be a worrier, especially when it comes to my children. I worry about their friends, their grades in school, where they will go to college, if they will go to college, who they will marry . . . Knowing this about me, I bet you can guess how difficult it is for me to live these verses in Philippians 4:6-7:

Don't worry about anything; instead, pray about everything. Tell God what you need, and thank him for all he has done. If you do this, you will experience God's peace, which is far more wonderful than the human mind can understand. His peace will guard your hearts and minds as you live in Christ Jesus.

I struggle to do this, but it helps me so much to write my prayers out or even just list out my prayer requests. I can look back and say, "I've already given that one to God. I don't need to take it back and worry about it. He's already on it."

Another way to guard your heart is to participate in a weekly worship service. Hebrews 10:25 says, "And let us not neglect our meeting together, as some people do, but encourage and warn each other, especially now that the day of his coming back again is drawing near." Occasionally, we all miss a worship service. Maybe our kids are playing in a basketball tournament or competing in a swim meet. Or maybe we make it to church, but we don't make it to church. For years, this was something we struggled with. We felt like we should be doing something *at* church, so we didn't actually make it *to* church. *Doing* ministry is a great excuse for missing a service. The number-one answer my staff and I (Craig) would give for missing a service was, "I need to be *doing* something else." Usually the *doing* was pretty important—tending to someone's need, ministering to a child, assisting with a program. You name it. The problem was, the more I missed a service, the harder it was to get to the next one.

Sometimes we get so busy that we cut out the very things that bring balance and focus into our lives. When you see yourself and your current life season against the backdrop of eternity, it becomes easier to make choices about how to spend your time. You may have to leave some things undone to get to a service. Don't cut corners here. Get to a service. By the way, going to church isn't just about learning or singing; it's also about fellowship with others—seeing friends, being with other believers, worshiping together.

The Internet has brought tremendous benefits to the church. I think it's a great opportunity to listen in to your church community while you are traveling or sick at home. Those who are thinking about attending your church may feel less apprehensive to show up after watching your church service online. However, the one thing the Internet can't provide is hand-to-hand, face-to-face, hug-to-hug, eye-to-eye fellowship—three-dimensional interaction, encouragement and support.

Finally, we have learned that guarding your heart includes listening to and participating in spiritual songs and worship. God not only *desires* us to worship Him, but He also *tells* us to worship Him: "Sing a new song to the LORD! Let the whole earth sing to the LORD!" (Ps. 96:1). God speaks to us through songs. When we praise the Lord, we see how big our God really is. Our focus transfers from our problems and onto our God. The magnitude of our great God makes our problems seem petty.

God has spoken to me (Mary) so many times through music. I can recall, as if it were yesterday, driving down the road with tears streaming down my cheeks, but at the same time singing to God these words from Mercy Me: "Hold fast, Help is on the way, Hold fast, He's come to save the day."[1] And the words from Casting Crowns: "And every tear I've cried, You hold in Your hand, You never left my side."[2] Songs like these have been a part of my life in a very real and powerful spiritual way. I feel like God has often used a song to speak straight to my soul and lift my spirits. Songs cut to the heart, especially when they are filled with truth from God's Word.

There is another memory that is etched in my heart of how music transcended an extremely difficult situation. I was walking into a hospital room with a close friend of mine to say goodbye to her 28-year-old son, who was on life support after an accidental fall. I wasn't prepared for what I was going to see, and I was praying for God to help me and to help my friends, Laura and Oran. When I walked into the room, I saw Brandon lying on the hospital bed with the most peaceful expression on his face. His girlfriend, Marie, was sitting next to him, holding his hand. Marie had set her iPod on Brandon's chest and the words from the song filled the room. It was as if God Himself were there in the room ministering to all of us through it. The lyrics were, "Why this happened I cannot explain, why write the script with such heartache and pain," and then the chorus, "My heart will fly, when I finally see you face to face, and my tears will fly away, away."[3]

Though we were all heartbroken, I had the most amazing peace knowing that Brandon would see Jesus that day and that we would see Brandon again someday. In the bigger picture, God had it all under control, even though we couldn't and still do not fully understand why. The song by Mercy Me felt as if it had been written for us that very day; and while I had heard it before, I had now experienced worship with that song at a completely different level. Those of us in the room with Brandon on that final day were worshiping God, thankful that it wasn't the end for Brandon and it wasn't the last time we would see Brandon. We knew that someday we would be worshiping the Lord together in heaven, not with an iPod, but with angels. Powerful heart and soul stuff can happen when we worship.

Our entire life depends on how we keep, guard and protect our heart. We will experience frustration or peace, turmoil or calm, agitation or quiet, grudges or forgiveness—all in direct correlation to how well we keep our heart or neglect it. How will you do this on your life's journey?

A Tale of Two, Maybe Three, Cities

Along the journey to a balanced life you will no doubt pass through several cities. Guarding your heart through some of them can be difficult. My goal was to end up in Authentis City with the whole family. We had seen pictures of it and heard it was a great place to not only visit but also to live. In fact, Mary and I had some friends move there a few years ago, and they say it's the best place to live . . . very family friendly. We were living in Toxis City at the time. We had only lived there for a few years, but it was enough time to embrace our surroundings yet not too much for it to really feel like home. It felt like there was another place for us somewhere.

There was a lot of noise where we used to live—very industrial, very loud and very dirty. Mary was sick a few times with an upper respiratory infection that got worse over time, each time. Our kids were frequently sick, and later we discovered that I was the carrier. I wasn't really watching my health. I would get ill, then pass it along to Mary and the kids. I guess I needed to wash my hands and cover my mouth more. Mary made several trips to the doctor's office with the kids during those years.

I can remember our neighbors, the Quicks. What a fun family to be around! They had moved here from Velos City, which is the city just north of us. You have to go through Velos City on your way to Toxis City if you are coming from the airport. The Quicks were always the life of the party. They were wired for energy, always smiling, but always in a hurry. Their kids played multiple sports, were in honors classes, and were super-involved with the youth group at church. I have never known a family to get so much done with so little time. We never really had quality time together with them, but they were always very nice to us.

There was something about Toxis City that we didn't want to leave behind. It could have been the friendships we developed, or maybe we were just afraid of change. Plus, you have to take all your stuff with you, and that means a lot of planning and packing. Probably it would have been easier to just put everyone in the car and leave, but we didn't; we couldn't. It was a lot of work though. We must have packed 200 boxes to get ready for the move. If it weren't for our friends Gregg and Janine, I'm not sure we would have been ready to leave when we did. They had moved to Authentis City a year previously, but we kept in touch through email and Facebook. They were part of the reason we wanted to move. Their life seemed to get better *after* they left Toxis City, and the whole family seemed happier, more content.

While they were helping us pack and load boxes, we realized we weren't going to be able to fit all of our stuff in the truck, so we had to make some hard decisions. What could we leave behind? What did we want to take with us? Was there anything we could just toss? It was great having Gregg and Janine helping us that day. It gave us some perspective on what we needed to take and what we needed to leave behind. We found out that it really is best to leave some of your stuff behind when you move. We probably tossed or left 50 to 70 boxes of stuff. "Travel light!" we now say.

We departed Toxis City on a Monday and got to Capas City later that evening. As we arrived in Capas City, everyone in the family was a little hungry, so we were looking for a place to stop and get something to eat. One of the kids pointed out a huge billboard on the side of the road. It was hilarious. I had to pull over and get a picture. I still have it on my phone. The sign said, "Stop Here! Don't Go Beyond Capas City Without Saying Hi!"

I had never driven through Capas City, but I had flown *over* Capas City so many times I felt like I had been there. I had been traveling a lot the last few years, so I would make the hour's drive through Velos City to the airport about four times a month. Driving through the city didn't really feel the same as flying over it. When you are over Capas City you would hardly recognize it. It seemed so small, contained and in order. I guess the higher up you are, the less movement you see below. We ended up stopping and grabbing something to eat at one of the local restaurants. Very nice people, great food and great banana cream pie! I think our family enjoyed being in Capas City more than I enjoyed being over it.

We left Capas City and continued our journey. We had been on the road for several hours without a stop for food or facilities. Everyone was feeling a bit cramped. Cam, Alec and Karimy were getting restless. Mary wanted me to pull over, and to make matters worse I had not been watching the GPS. We were off course. I rarely ask for directions. I'm a guy, and we don't do that. I saw a sign up ahead. As I tried to drown out the sounds of discontent from the backseat, I could barely make out the name of the city we had inadvertently detoured to; it was Audas City.

No, we didn't stop here. Why? Because *I* didn't want to. Yes, the rest of the family was hungry. Yes, we all needed to use the facilities, and no I wasn't willing to admit it was my fault for getting lost. After all, I am the one driving while everyone else is texting, watching a video, playing on their iPod, reading their Kindle or sleeping. I am the one trying to keep my eyes open and not fall asleep. I am the one who is sacrificing. I am the one making sure everyone's needs are met. *How about a little thanks,* I thought.

I drove recklessly through Audas City until I was forced to slow down by my friends at the Highway Patrol. This made matters worse. "Dad, you are in trouble," was the chorus from the back. This only made me more upset. Mary didn't say a word; she just looked at me with her arms crossed. Even though she didn't say anything I knew she was right, but I couldn't admit it.

The officer walked up and asked me the question I had heard a few times before: "Do you know how fast you were going?" This wasn't the time for sarcasm, however much I wanted to let it flow. Instead, I just apologized for my speed and arrogant disregard for personal or family safety. I told him we were headed for Authentis City and I took a wrong turn about 30 miles ago, and that's how we ended up here in Audas City. The officer's response wasn't what I expected. He told me he talks to at least five people a day who miss that turnoff. "It's easy to miss," he said.

He handed back my license and said, "I'm going to forgive you for this one; just do a U-turn right here." He pointed with his hand. "And head back to where you missed the turnoff. Have a good rest of your journey."

I said, "Thanks," rolled up the window and breathed a sigh of relief. I couldn't afford another ticket, or gift certificate, as my kids were now calling them. I pulled out slowly, made the U-turn and headed back to the missed turnoff. From the back of the car I could hear, "Dad, you are so lucky!" They were probably right. I deserved a consequence for my arrogance. Before I could say anything, Cameron said, "It's a good thing they allow U-turns in Audas City," to which Mary added, "I know, right?"

We finally made it back to the turnoff for Authentis City. We were all pretty tired and hungry at this point, and we needed to get out and stretch, so we took the first off-ramp we could find. The sign said Gas-Food-

Lodging, and we were looking for all three. We got some gas for the car, food for the stomach and headed to the hotel for some sleep.

We woke up the next morning refreshed and ready to go. We walked outside and got in the car, excited to continue our journey. I put the key in the ignition and . . . nothing. What? Wait, maybe I left it in neutral. No, it's in gear, let me try it again. I turned the key and . . . nothing. The car wouldn't start. Dead battery? Dead starter? Something worse? It's amazing how fast your attitude can sink when things aren't going your way. I opened the hood as if I knew what I was doing. I didn't. I started to look on my phone for a place to repair the car. It looked like there was a place about two miles away, so I gave them a call. "Tenas City Auto Repair, may I help you?" said a nice voice over the telephone.

"Hi, yeah, uh, I need some help with our car." To make a long story short, we had the car towed to the repair center. The mechanic said he could fix it but he didn't have the part. He let us know that he would have it first thing in the morning.

"Great," I said sarcastically. *Another night in Tenas City.*

It's amazing how stuff like this doesn't really bother kids. They looked at it like it was an adventure. "Cool, we can check this place out!" exclaimed Alec. "Is there a mall?" said Karimy. "Can we go back to that pizza place?" asked Cameron. Mary was excited about the adventure as well. I guess it's all in how you look at it. I won't lie to you. Fifteen hours and $523.45 later, and that wasn't even counting the car repair, we pulled out. It took some persistence from all of us while in Tenas City not to mention the occasional attitude check.

We weren't too far from Authentis City at this point. We were all playing a game that Karimy made up. Something about "I'm going on a trip and . . ." We were all laughing and joking around. Alec started in with one of his rhymes that he pulls out of nowhere; Cameron was talking a mile a minute in one of his made-up voices; and Karimy was talking to Mary about a new recipe she wanted to try. I just continued to drive, with a smile on my face, hoping and praying that our lives together as a family in Authentis City would be a destination worthy of the journey.

Try That on for Size

As we travel through life, the one city that could quite possibly give us the biggest challenge is audacity. Audacity is that pride or bold arrogance that puts us in direct opposition to God. "God opposes the proud but gives grace to the humble" (Jas 4:6, *NIV*). Do you know that this is one of only two times in the New Testament where we are told that God is in opposition to us? The next time we see this language is in 1 Peter 5:5. Both of these verses are referencing Proverbs 3:34, which says, "He has no use for conceited people, but shows favor to those who are humble" (*TEV*). All of this suggests one thing: When we are proud, when we are arrogant, when we are full of conceit, God "sets Himself in battle array against us!"[4]

I don't want to stand across from God who is in full battle gear and in attack position, looking solely and squarely at me. Apparently, this is a pretty important issue with our Lord if He is ready to go to battle with us on this. James is saying that every time we have a thought or action that puts ourselves above others, we are being arrogant and, as a result, God is in direct opposition to us. He is against us; He resists us.

I don't know if you have ever had anyone resist you. If you have children, enough said. I think my best shot at illustrating resistance is with our dog, Holiday. She is a Golden Retriever, and the best dog on the planet. In fact, she is sitting at my feet right now as I write this chapter. If I move, she moves. If I leave, she walks me to the door. If I sit down on the floor, she is right there next to me. I don't mean across the room next to me. I mean right up against me, next to me. When we all come home, she will pass Mary, Cameron, Alec and Karimy and wait for me to come in the door. I'm not going to lie to you; I am her favorite. (I hope that wasn't prideful.) Anyway, I tell you this story so you get to know my dog's personality.

She is a great dog and will follow me anywhere . . . until I try to give her a bath. Now, let me remind you, she is a Retriever—she likes to go in the water. She jumps in the pool all the time. However, when I roll out the hose and bring out the shampoo, she freezes. You can call her and coax her, but in the end, you will have to push, drag or carry her from where she is to where she needs to be. She resists by stopping, dropping and rolling on her side. Her resistance is a passive resistance. She doesn't growl, show her teeth or put up a fight. She just shows her resistance by lying down. She is no help when she is in full resistance mode.

Now, can you imagine God in full resistance mode? You think bathing a 75-pound Golden Retriever is tough? Try arrogance and pride with your Maker. Arrogance and pride have no place in your life. Unfortunately, arrogance will raise its ugly head from time to time, usually when someone compliments you or you do something extraordinary, and that little voice says, "Wow, that was pretty good. How awesome are you!" It's not the voice that makes you arrogant. That's the attack. It's when you start believing it that you cross the line.

Attacks from the enemy are rarely head-on. They are subtle temptations or voices that over time wear you down, and then the enemy has you right where he wants you. When those thoughts pop into your head, break that agreement immediately. Pray out loud, "God, my desire is to be Your humble servant. I do not want to be an arrogant person. I am a child of God who, through the power of the Holy Spirit, was used to make a difference in somebody's life today. I renounce, in the name of Jesus Christ of Nazareth, the thoughts in my mind that are causing me to focus on myself."

Since God opposes the proud, I often think, "Is God ever not resisting me?" I mean, it seems like all I think about is me and what I want or what I need. The root of all sin is arrogance; so is it a no-win battle? Of course not. But it is a continual struggle.

I (Mary) know how easy it is for women to compare themselves to others. I am constantly looking at women I see on magazine covers, on television or even in real life. I compare myself to my friends and think, *She is skinnier than me; she is prettier than me; she is more organized than me; she is a better teacher than me; she's a more patient mom than me.* The list continues as I see my own faults and other people's gifts or talents. I can start to feel downright depressed in who I am or who I have become.

The reverse is also true, I am sad to say. Sometimes, I hear a compliment, and that compliment swirls around in my head and I begin to look down on them. I begin to think I'm better in one way or another than that person. Maybe my boss at work has said something to me about the previous person in my job and I think to myself something like, *I would never do that.* Or maybe it's my kids or my husband who give me a compliment, and I think, *That's right, I am a pretty good cook, or a pretty good mom.*

Is it possible to be confident and self-assured and know that you can or did do a good job, but not be arrogant about it? Yes, it's possible, but we must be cautious. Humility isn't thinking about yourself less; it's thinking about God more. It's the approach of John the Baptist that can best keep us on track, when he said, "He must become greater and greater, and I must become less and less" (John 3:30). Here's where we need to give the credit where the credit is due. Did God give you that talent? Did

He allow you to be successful or beautiful or well known or whatever good that you have in you? Of course He did. And He can just as easily take that away from you. Praise Him and give Him the credit. Allow your life to bring glory to God and not yourself.

First Peter 5:5 tells us, "Clothe yourselves with humility toward one another" (*NASB*). To clothe yourself with humility doesn't mean that you need to reduce your wardrobe. What the verse is saying is that we literally need to dress ourselves—our words, thoughts and actions—with humility; we need to put on humility. This verse gives us all hope. Yes, some of us may not have a great wardrobe, but there is hope for those of us who don't have a good eye for spiritual fashion.

I don't know if you have ever watched the show on TLC, *What Not to Wear*. It's a show that will secretly videotape people who are not at the top of their fashion game, and then confront them unsuspectingly about their wardrobe and offer them $5,000 for a new wardrobe. There is a catch. The fashion criminal must learn to "dress" differently, using some guidelines given to them by the co-hosts of the show, and they must surrender their entire current wardrobe to the fashion police to be disposed of forever. Once the candidates agree, they are off to New York for a wardrobe makeover.

My wife and I watch the show from time to time, laughing while saying, "Do those people really think they look good in that?" Anyway, the end of the show is always the same. The fashion criminals have surrendered all their old clothes, gone through a minor emotional crisis and have then *put on* the new clothes they have purchased with the help of the co-hosts. Once all this transpires, the person returns home for an unveiling party to see the transformation that has taken place. Usually, it's quite remarkable. In the final moments of the show, you get to see side-by-side pictures of the before and after wardrobes. The difference is considerable.

Come to think of it, the show *What Not to Wear* could be the title of a show using 1 Peter 5:5 as the premise. Could you imagine someone secretly videotaping us walking around town clothed in our arrogant outbursts and selfish ambitions? That alone could bring us to a humble reality. The great reminder for all of us is this: If we do get caught wearing that prideful wardrobe, we can always take it off, throw it away and put on something more presentable—*humility*. Take that into the dressing room to see if it fits. It felt a bit snug to me, but Mary said it looks great. She also said I could wear it year round. How awesome is that!

ACT ACCORDINGLY

Everything on earth has its own time and its own season.
ECCLESIASTES 3:1, *CEV*

Hey, Jesus Was Single

Has anyone ever told you, "Act your age"? It has been said to me. What the very well-meaning person is saying when he or she aims these words at you is that you should behave a bit more maturely than you are currently behaving. Your life experience, education and lessons learned up to this point require that you act differently than a child would act. In a sense, they are saying, "Could you please act accordingly?"

If a situation calls for you to be quiet and contrite, you don't bounce in full of life and energy, telling jokes. Why? It's not appropriate. Likewise, it would put a significant damper on a party if you walked in with a sad and quiet demeanor, complaining about what a terrible day you just had. It's not appropriate. In fact, we are reminded in Ecclesiastes 3:1: "There is a time for everything, a season for every activity under heaven."

We live in a world full of seasons that mandate certain changes for us. You can't have summer and winter at the same time. You have summer, *then* you have fall, *then* you have winter, *then* you have spring. Seasons change. Seasons are visible and predictable. Our behavior changes depending on the season we are in.

Let's apply the idea of seasonality to ourselves. When we are born, we are at the mercy of others who take care of us. We depend upon them for everything from clean clothes and diapers to food and entertainment. We move on to preschool, then to elementary school, then to middle school and high school; then on to college or the workplace.

In our early twenties, we are single and ready to mingle. Our time is our time. We can do what we want to do, when we want to do it. When we get up in the morning and leave for work or school, we aren't leaving anyone behind at home. When work or school is finished for the day, we can go home and watch TV, go out and hang with friends, or volunteer our time in a worthwhile cause.

When you get married, and if you have children, you can't live a seasonally single life. If you do try to live a seasonally single life, you will probably end up being seasonally single again. Of course, when you get married, you move into a new season of life. You are more responsible with how you spend your time. You simply can't say yes to everything you would like to or could say yes to. Why? Because you have new responsibilities at home. Your spouse needs your time, attention and love. That necessitates spending less time at your job or saying yes to other interests and other people.

Paul says in 1 Corinthians 7:32-34, "In everything you do, I want you to be free from the concerns of this life. An unmarried man can spend his time doing the Lord's work and thinking how to please him. But a married man can't do that so well. He has to think about his earthly responsibilities and how to please his wife. His interests are divided. In the same way, a woman who is no longer married or has never been married can be more devoted to the Lord in body and in spirit, while the married woman must be concerned about her earthly responsibilities and how to please her husband." When we are married, we need to act accordingly. It's our *season*.

As time goes on, you and your spouse may be blessed with children. Mary and I were blessed with multiples, and then went on to adopt! We know how it feels when you add kids to the mix. Responsibilities also get multiplied! This is truly a season of responsibility, not at work, but at home. Your family must take the front seat in your "car," and your job must take the backseat. Why? Because you are replaceable at work. At home, you are not. At work, there are others to fill your shoes if something comes up. At home, no one else can be a spouse to your mate. No one else can be a mom or a dad to your children.

Besides being single, married without children or married with children at home, there are other seasons you might encounter as well. You might be single with kids, or married with kids out of the home—empty nesters. The different seasons of our lives demand that we act accordingly. When we don't live life within its correct seasonal balance, life becomes hectic in no time at all. A correct life PACE is the key to healthy living.

With that in mind, let me remind you that Jesus was *single*, with no kids. When I hear people say, "I want to do ministry just like Jesus did," I want to ask them what season of life they are in. I just can't picture my wife saying, "Okay, hun, I will see you in a few days. Have fun with the 12 guys on your trip. When will you be back? Oh, you don't know? That's okay. I'll take care of the kids and the house while you are gone."

Jesus had a season of life that allowed Him to fulfill His mission. If you are married, you simply can't do ministry at the pace Jesus did. You have other responsibilities at home, with your spouse and kids.

I think it's important to note that I'm not saying it's wrong to travel with your job. I'm not talking about being gone for work, on occasion, to provide for your family. I am talking about repeatedly neglecting your family's interests because you are living your life out of its current season by overworking at your job or cramming your calendar with everything people ask you to do. Your job may require you to travel, and that necessitates being away from your spouse and your children from time to time. Mine does, so I understand that. But when this happens, how does one live in his or her season, keep his job and keep his family relationships healthy?

These are not prescriptions to the problem, but I want to share some ways that Mary and I deal with periodic departures related to life and work. The first is to build in some family time when I return. We usually do this by hanging out and watching a movie, going to a favorite restaurant or playing games. We try to reconnect and fill each other in on what happened while we were apart from each other.

While I am away, I want to make sure they are getting the message that I miss them, that they are important to me and that I am thinking about them. So I make an effort to call and talk to each of the kids at least once a day. If they are at home, we use iChat and FaceTime so we can actually see each other. This usually turns into a hilarious experience when I rotate the computer around to show the family my hotel room or where I am speaking. The next thing I know, Mary is holding up her cat, or Alec has his hamster, and the dog is barking at me through the screen. It's a three-ring circus, but we all feel connected, and that helps all of us. It's not the real thing, but it's a suitable substitute when one of us is away.

You Can't Do That

Now let's address life's priorities in the context of each season and show how a person's priorities may be seasonally healthy or unhealthy.

Example Number One: A 22-year-old single college graduate goes overseas to serve as a missionary for two years. He eats, drinks, breathes and sleeps ministry. He finds time for personal enrichment and play, but ministry is taking the majority of his time. Seasonally, this works for him. His seasonal priorities are balanced.

Example Number Two: A 32-year-old married ministry veteran with three kids, whose ages are 4, 8 and 11, decides to take on additional roles and responsibilities in her already hurried life without removing any other role or responsibility. Seasonally, this *may not* work for her family. She *is* married, she *does* have children, so her seasonal priorities may be out of balance.

Example Number Three: A 45-year-old man, divorced with no children, occasionally spends 9- to 11-hour days at the office and, from time to time, goes in on the weekend to finish projects. On weekends, he plays in a soccer league, volunteers in the church worship band and hangs out with his friends. He finds time to work out daily and watches what he eats. Seasonally, this works for him. In essence, he is married to his job, but his long work hours don't take away from his relationships and his health, because he has learned to schedule in downtime on the weekend. He makes time for his spiritual and relational growth.

Example Number Four: A 65-year-old widow, with eight grandkids, volunteers at the hospital on the weekends. She watches her two youngest grandchildren Monday through Friday so her daughter can teach school. On weeknights, she is involved in playing bridge, attends a Bible Study, participates in a quilting club and is a mentor for the young mothers' group at her church. In her "spare" time, she attends her grandkids' sporting and school events, goes to doctor and dentist appointments, and makes meals for the sick and homebound. Whenever the women's ministry needs a volunteer, she is the first one to sign up. This could be an example of an overcommitted, hectic lifestyle, which develops when a caring person cannot say no to an opportunity. This is also a life lived out of its current season.

I'm not sure where I (Craig) picked it up, but I really thought I was here to change the world. Perhaps it's my personality, my birth order or my arrogance that got me to believe that myth. The reality is that they all contributed to an unhealthy and unbalanced life. What a relief to understand that maybe I should just be playing a role in changing the world and not be the lightning rod for it! Maybe I just needed to do what God has called me to do, and that's it. What if everyone did only what God has called him or her to do, and that was it? Perhaps we would all have a more balanced life.

Here's some advice I wish I had given myself 10 years ago: "If you want to change the world, start at home and work out from there." I was reminded of this as I was looking through some of my kids' old school papers from kindergarten. I came across these words on a half-decorated piece of construction paper with a crayon marked name . . .

"Walk a little slower, daddy,"
Said a child so small.
"I'm following in your footsteps
And I don't want to fall.

Sometimes your steps are very fast
Sometimes they're hard to see
So walk a little slower, daddy
For you are leading me.

Someday when I'm all grown up
You're what I want to be;
Then I will have a little child
Who'll want to follow me.

And I would want to lead just right
And know that I was true;
So walk a little slower, daddy,
For I must follow you."
(Author Unknown)

I observed this dilemma the other day. I watched something look at everything and do nothing. I have learned that doing everything was really something, so seeing something look at everything and doing nothing was discouraging. I have also seen something doing everything, and that really was tiring, even depressing. Seeing everything doing nothing was disappointing; and seeing something doing everything was discouraging. Bottom line, I didn't like watching everything do nothing, and I didn't like watching something do everything. Perhaps it's best to ignore nothing, see everything and just do something.

I don't have to do it all. I *can't* do everything, but I can do something, and that something should start at home.

Doesn't Everyone Play Soccer on Saturday?

There is a league of soccer players here in Southern California that caters to youth. They have a great program that builds skill and teamwork. Our kids played in this league when they were younger, and they thoroughly enjoyed their experience. In fact, as parents, we have enjoyed watching our kids play, practice and build friendships over the years. The league is usually identified by their initials—AYSO. While our kids were playing in this league, we would joke, saying the initials stood for All Your Saturdays Occupied because, well, they were. Games were always played on Saturdays, with practice during the week.

Now multiply the soccer times of three kids with how many other sports or activities they are involved in. Youth group, church, volunteering, swimming, basketball, birthday parties. You can see where this is going. There was a time when our boys were in karate. We loved the respect, honor and discipline that karate taught them. What was difficult was the daily, more-than-an-hour practice after school. Mary would pick the boys up from school, get them a snack and changed into their gear and onto the dojo mat before four o'clock. I understand sports and the value of teaching teamwork, positive attitude and discipline. However, it certainly adds a bit of a strain on the family and can get hectic if you have more than one child.

Our three children are vastly different from each other. They all like different sports. There was a time when Cameron was on a swim team, Alec was playing lacrosse and Karimy was finishing up soccer and going into basketball season. We were scrambling to get carpools together just so we could drop off and pick up at three different locations on time. We had no time to eat dinner as a family since practice times overlapped. The weekends were filled with swim meets, lacrosse games, soccer and basketball games, leaving us to wonder how single parents survive having their kids in any sports at all.

We had to make some changes in our lifestyle. We have tried our best to commit to two things: dinner together as a family and one sport at a time per child. Yes, you are correct in assuming this was not a popular decision in our family, because it wasn't enforced by most of the families in our neighborhood or in our particular area of the country. "But Kathy's mom let's her play volleyball, soccer, basketball, softball, do gymnastics, dance, checkers, chess, twister, Girl Scouts, choir . . . and she plays an instrument; so why do I get to only play one sport at a time?"

Okay, first, "We don't argue with 11-year-olds." Second, and as parents, we have all said it, "We're not Kathy's parents. Would you like to go live with Kathy?"

It was hard for our kids to understand why they couldn't do more than one sport at a time. We explained that different families have different rules and fewer kids! What works for one family doesn't work for another. Helping our kids understand this continues to be at least a twice-a-year conversation.

You might be saying, *That's not right. You are holding her back from using all of her God-given potential.* Yeah, maybe we are. But we are doing the best we can with what we have now. We like to think that we are teaching our children the importance of choosing their activities carefully and pacing their calendar and life so that they have downtime, free time and, most importantly, time with God and family.

I (Mary) posted a question on Facebook recently and asked my friends how many sports they thought were enough for one child to participate in. I was somewhat surprised by the answers I received. Most people who answered subscribed to the one sport per kid at a time rule. I really liked what my friend Stacey had to say. She summed it up this way: "I think it depends on the individual child and the family. Are there a lot of kids? Do both parents work outside the home? Do the kids bicker and cause problems when bored or under-exercised? Is the home stressful and chaotic? Will too many activities be the straw that breaks the poor camel's back? Can we afford it? Can my child drive himself or herself? I like one sport and one church activity per kid at a time. Soccer and small-group Bible study, as an example."

The key is balance. If your church offers five small groups, three connection points and seven activities during the week, do you need to be at all of them? The answer may be different for each family. For us, the answer is no, we do not need to be at all of them. If there is a youth event happening at church, we do make it a priority to try to get our kids there. The reason for this is that it supports our value of God being the center of our life. But don't get that confused with church being the center of our life. Great youth leaders who build into our kids, and friends they can connect with who challenge them to a deeper understanding of who Christ is and how they can live out that value in their life, are indispensable in our family. We know firsthand the value of what other leaders in ministry can add to a child or student's life. We want our kids to be a part of that. We want them to hear the same things we have been telling them, but from another adult in another context. Activities such as small-group studies, overnighters, camps and youth services on the weekend are a priority; but like sports, it's easy to overdo it. Balance is the key.

This brings us back to the different seasons in life. If you have only one child and he or she needs to stay busy, and you don't work outside the home, then you are in a different season than a family with multiple kids and two parents who work outside the home. The idea is to take a look at the needs of *your* family. Identify the season *your* family is in and make decisions that will keep you all healthy.

It's okay to go against the flow if that is what you need to do. It's not easy, but it is doable. At least there is someone—two someones—behind the words of this book who is with you and for you! Maybe, just maybe, together we can support and encourage each other to a more balanced life.

11

COME
TOGETHER

One thing for sure, if you ever see a turtle on top of a fencepost,
you know he had help getting there.
ALEX HALEY

Come Together with Your Spouse

How do you feel when you are with your spouse? Do you feel like you are on the same wavelength? Or do you feel like you are on parallel train tracks traveling at different speeds and with different destinations and stops along the way? I (Mary) remember feeling like that most of the time.

At the beginning of each year, Craig would make a list of goals that he wanted to accomplish that year. They all pertained to ministry, mission and advancement of personal goals. I used to make a list of goals as well. There was a goal for each of our kids, goals for our marriage and goals for us as a family. We both set out at the beginning of the year with different "destinations" in mind, and invariably that caused conflict in our relationship.

While in counseling, Jim gave us homework from time to time. After we had worked with him for a while and we felt like things were going well, Jim told us to go on a date and review our marriage. *Huh?* He asked us to answer these three specific questions in regard to our relationship and marriage.

1. What was negative and upside down in the past?
2. What is positive and going well now?
3. What do we want to do, build or add to our relationship?

He told us to set aside time—to actually put it on the calendar six months later to pull out our answers to those questions and review them. And then he said something that really stuck with me: "It's not an accident when things are going badly, and it's not an accident when things are going well." It's important to live *intentionally* in our marriage! It's like the drift principal we talked about in chapter 4. If you are not paddling toward something in your marriage, then you are drifting. Or another way to say it is, "If you are coasting in your marriage, then you are going downhill."

While writing this book, I looked back on our notes describing that first time we met to review the three questions. I still remember everything about that evening. We had a baby-sitter for our kids so we could take our time and have the privacy we needed to talk openly. We decided to go to a coffee shop rather than a restaurant, since we knew it could take awhile to get through the questions. We were sitting outside of the coffee shop next to a fire pit, sipping tea lattes, yet I was shivering. I wasn't shivering because I was cold, but because I was nervous. What would happen when we seriously sat down and went over these things? I was afraid that if we were truly honest, we might hurt each other's feelings and end up in an argument.

I remember sharing that nervousness with Craig and telling him I was afraid of how this was going to turn out. He took my hands and prayed with me, asking God to guide us as we talked, thanking Him for intervening in our marriage and bringing us closer than ever before. I felt the old weight of fear fall from my back as we said amen. I want to share with you some of the things we wrote that night.

What was negative and upside down? I didn't feel loved and valued by Craig. We had no real family time. We didn't know how to share our feelings. Craig was not home and was overworking. When Craig was home, he was not present with us. Craig didn't help around the house or with the kids; he just played with them. Our pace was too fast. We had no joy. We focused on the wrong things. I was resentful; Craig had a short fuse. We were not honest with each other. We "faked" acting like things were okay to other people. We rarely took a vacation. We were bitter toward others. The spiritual side of our relationship was missing. We never prayed together, except at meals.

What was positive now? Mary feels loved and valued. There are more flowers and notes and even "I love yous." Craig wants to be at home. We are talking more to each other about how we feel. We pray together regularly. There is more time spent with the whole family. Bike rides, playing catch and swimming with the kids. Craig is much less angry. There is honesty and openness in our conversations. Craig is helping out around the house and with the kids' homework. We have a more manageable schedule and pace of life. More grace with family and others. We are able to "put self in other's shoes" rather than get angry. We extend forgiveness toward those who have offended us. There is JOY! Disagreements are not turning into arguments that last for days. We are looking forward to scheduled vacations together.

What do we want to do, build, or add to our relationship? Go to a marriage conference together. Take three vacations or mini-vacations a year. Craig will read a marriage book. We will speak together at conferences and share what we have learned. We will have a date night once a week. No ruts! Work out together. Share with each other what God is teaching us individually. More backrubs. (Craig) More flowers! (Me) Consistent monitoring of our family schedule for balance (and cushion).

That was our first time doing the exercise. We had a pretty big difference from where we had started to where we were at review time. These changes were not easy. It required weekly counseling appointments and purposeful discussions and changes. It meant saying no to opportunities that came up for either of us, and our kids. We did things that initially felt very uncomfortable, like talking about our feelings or praying aloud together or even helping with homework. The next time we did the exercise, we found that we had gotten a little off track on some things and that other things were still going okay. We were surprised that we had accomplished some of the things we wanted to do as a couple, but we still had a ways to go.

The opposite of being connected is being disconnected. "Disconnected" is an important word to us. When we get too busy and things start to get hectic in our life, our relationship becomes less "together" and more disconnected. I (Mary) usually am the first one to feel this. It's important at that point that I go to Craig and tell him that I am beginning to feel disconnected from him. That's not anything we ignore and simply hope it gets better. That is a warning sign for us, and we need to take it seriously. It's time to get away and get connected on a date night. When we do this it interrupts possible drift. We become more focused and intentional about how we keep a healthy marriage.

Maybe you are feeling like that right now with your spouse. How do you become intentional in your marriage? You might start by asking a few questions like the ones we came up with:

1. How are you feeling about your week?
2. What was the highlight of your week? Why?
3. What one thing has God been showing you this week?
4. Who are your three closest friends? Why?
5. Where do you think we have the most conflict as a couple? How can this be helped?
6. How should we handle conflict in our marriage?
7. What would be your favorite date night if money were no object?
8. What would be your favorite date night if we had only $20 to spend?
9. Why did you marry me? ("Because I love you" is not an answer.)
10. If I wanted to buy you a small gift once a month, what would you like it to be?

11. If you could pick one book to read together, what book would it be?
12. What is the best way for me to show you how much I love you?
13. Where would you like to go on vacation? Why?
14. Where do you see us as a couple in 10 years, 20 years, 50 years?

Come Together with Your Friends

In Ecclesiastes 4:9-10, Solomon tells us, "You are better off to have a friend than to be all alone, because then you will get more enjoyment out of what you earn. If you fall, your friend can help you up. But if you fall without having a friend nearby, you are really in trouble."

Over the past 20 years, I've observed something about the springtime. This is the time when churches are prone to hold retreats—men's retreats, women's retreats, couples' retreats, pastors' wives retreats. I like retreats. It is an "acceptable" time to stop work, slow down and just relax with some great people. If planned far enough in advance, even the busiest of people will show up to a retreat. That included me (Mary). I literally needed a retreat to tell me it was okay to stop working and connect with other women.

I had a girlfriend I could never seem to find the time to hang out with, but we were old standby retreat friends. We had been on staff together since we were pregnant with our boys, and we were comfortable with each other. It was great to be able to catch up and find out what was going on in each other's families, our lives and to hear about what our guys were up to in their separate ministry areas. We would connect a bit, swap stories and marvel at the similarities we never knew existed. We would question why we didn't get together more often during the year and promise that this year, we would get together more often. Then the retreat would end, life would go back to its crazy "normal" and, before we knew it, it was retreat time again.

Fast forward a few years, and I am at a new church and in a new season of my life. I have a friend who is also a pastor's wife, but we have a different kind of friendship. When I first met her, we connected right away. We had a lot of things in common, as well as both of us growing up as a PK (pastor's kid). However, things quickly became uncomfortable for me when she challenged me to go deeper as a friend. I carried around some past "friendship hurts" and even betrayals and had learned to keep a safe distance from friends. For many years, I never really took the time to be a good friend. And being a good friend certainly does take time. I was too busy to go to the next level in any friendship outside of ministry. In fact, my closest girlfriends were those I directly worked with in some type of ministry capacity.

I limited myself in my friendships with others for a few reasons. The first reason was because I was literally too busy to have close friends. My hectic lifestyle left no room for fun with friends. The second reason corresponded closely with the first. I was afraid that if I let someone into my life, I would get hurt again. Time and time again, I would get close to someone who would move away. I didn't want to open myself up to that pain again. The last reason was because I was afraid to be vulnerable and truthful with someone. I guess I had trust issues. If I shared what things were really like at home, I would be giving that friend information she could use to hurt me. If word got out that my husband and I didn't get along well, and that my kids were less than perfect, what would happen next? Would Craig lose his job? Would we lose our ministries? So I dealt with these fears by keeping most of my friends at a comfortable distance. Going deeper in a friendship requires not only trust, but also openness, honesty, authenticity—letting another person see the real you, scars and all.

When Debbie challenged me to go deeper, I wasn't sure I was ready for that. But I felt God nudging me toward a relationship like that. I had just reread the book *Captivating*, and I was struck by these words: "God invites us to risk trusting him and enter into redemptive friendships with others—to open ourselves up to the possibility of being hurt as well as to the possibility of tasting the sweet fruit of companionship."[1] So I made a conscious decision to let her in, and do you know what happened? We became great friends in a short amount of time because both of us let down our guards and put forth the effort it takes to be real.

What I also found out when I took the risk to be vulnerable with others was that they didn't judge me, but actually could *relate* to me. A couple of gals even shared with me that they used to be intimidated by me. What? Intimidated by *moi*? Why? Well, maybe it was because I had a Mary Poppins, practically perfect, stage personality going on. Who wants to be friends with someone like that? Not me.

Some friends don't help, but a true friend is closer than your own family (Prov. 18:24, *CEV*).

What kind of friend are you? Are you a retreat friend, or a year-round friend? Are you willing to be real with someone else and share your feelings, be accountable and take risks year-round? I would challenge you to do that. Friends are one of God's greatest blessings. We weren't made to go it alone! In *Captivating: Unveiling the Mystery of a Woman's Soul*, John and Stasi Eldredge write, "The capacity of a woman's heart for meaningful relationships is vast. There is no way your husband or your children can ever provide the intimacy and relational satisfaction you need. A woman must have women friends."[2]

Get involved in a Bible study, or if there isn't one where you can be real, start one in your home and invite the friends you want to get to know better. Or join a scrapbook group or Bunco group or MOPS group or book club. Do whatever you need to do to avoid being isolated from other women. But then take it a step further and let your guard down and be real with those friends. Be the initiator in the relationship and pursue friendship by inviting your friend to do things with you, sending a thoughtful card or email, picking up a small gift for your friend when you are away, and offering to help her whenever you can.

Come Together with Others

Just because you live in a fishbowl and get along with everyone doesn't mean you are connected with others on a deeper level. Yes, it does take courage to connect.

The devil attacks you by isolating you! When the Bible talks about the devil roaming around like a roaring lion seeking someone to devour (see 1 Pet. 5:8), it is not painting a picture of passivity.

If you have ever seen a documentary on animals in Africa, it will usually involve a herd of wildebeest, antelope or gazelle trying to cross a river. They approach tentatively, at first, then one jumps in and then another. Soon the entire herd is swimming with all they've got to get across the current. Once across and tired, the lion looks for the weakest one of the herd, not in the front mind you, but in the back. The lion waits for one to be isolated from the rest—the one who is most tired, most defenseless, the one who has been separated from the others. Lions aren't just brawn; they are brains too. They don't attack the strongest in the middle of the herd with the protection of all their wildebeest friends around them. No, they attack the one that will put up the least resistance, or worse, doesn't even see it coming. The scene plays out as the lion waits for the right moment, then attacks. It is ruthless and aggressive, and there is no chance for this isolated and helpless member of the herd. There is a reason "all the believers met together constantly and shared everything they had" (Acts 2:44). There is safety in numbers!

As we have traveled around the country sharing our story, our mistakes, our near divorce and the things we have learned from all of this, we have found one thing to be true in every single city we've visited. There were others there who had been in our shoes, had walked the same path, had made big mistakes, felt enormous pain or were currently in a difficult situation. Craig and I shared with them our belief that "We are all messed up and in need of Jesus." We found comfort in knowing that we weren't alone, and they found the same.

We were surprised to hear how many of these people, our newfound friends, had never shared their story with anyone. They found the courage to tell us, because we were safe. We had risked first, and they were following our lead. We passed out cards and asked them to write down something they were going to ask God to do for them, to write down their prayer request. It could be something in their marriage, their family, their ministry, their job or wherever they needed God's healing touch. Here are some of the things they wrote:

> "My husband and I are struggling to find purpose and attachment in our marriage. We are so emotionally detached most times. We need God's healing."

> "Lord, I want you to protect my marriage and help me be a balanced mom and wife."

> "I need connection in my life, to my life. Connection in my marriage. Connection to my God. I want to be accountable and responsible with my life. I want to be intentional."

> "I wish my husband would engage himself in my life and the lives of our kids."

> "I have been given another chance (by my wife) for our marriage and by my God in ministry. I want to be right this time."

"Thanks to marriage counseling and prayer, and the support of amazing friends, I finally feel one with my husband, and I know I am very loved."

"I feel enormous guilt as a woman in ministry that I'm either short-changing my family by giving my all for God, or I am short-changing God by giving Him less of myself because I need to take care of my family."

"I'm addicted to busyness and can't relax to spend time with my kids."

"I have been putting ministry before my family. I need to take my wife out on a date and spend quality time with my kids."

"I spend more time with people at church than I do with my own kids and family."

"Our family is drifting apart. It's difficult not to bring work home (that's for both of us), and we need to close the gap!"

"I want to be more available to my family than I am to my staff at work."

"I want to become the spiritual leader in my family that causes my wife to feel secure and my kids to choose Jesus!"

"I'm a workaholic. I don't have any close friends other than my wife. My whole happiness and identity is in my job, working 60 hours a week."

"I am a workaholic. I need to change. I want a happy home!"

"I've tried so hard to make everyone believe that I'm perfect that I'm scared to death to slip and for people to find out who I really am."

"I am popular, but I feel I have no REAL friends. I feel lonely a lot and would love a friend. I love my husband, but I'd also like a friend who knows the REAL me."

"Heal my fear of failure. Heal my worry of *Am I doing enough?*"

We were amazed by the vulnerability of those who shared their struggle and pain. We prayed for every single person as we read through these cards. We had asked them to leave their names off the cards and remain anonymous, but we so wished that we could connect with them again on a one-to-one basis.

How can we as Christ-followers—all part of one family—love each other unconditionally, no matter what we have done in our past? Maybe we could start by looking in the mirror before pointing our finger at someone else. Maybe we could stop grading the seriousness of the sins of others and put more time in removing the proverbial log from our own eye. Satan tries to disconnect us from each other by tempting us to compare ourselves with others' faults? It's never healthy. It either makes us feel better than others or worse about ourselves. Satan knows that we are better together, and God desires unity, encouragement and love among His followers.

Hebrews 10:24-25 urges us, "Let us think about each other and help each other to show love and do good deeds. You should not stay away from the church meetings, as some are doing, but you should meet together and encourage each other. Do this even more as you see the day coming" (*NCV*). We should connect regularly with other Christians; and instead of putting them down or "kicking them out," we should love them and help them.

This led us to the idea to start a Christian e-community that could span across state lines, and country lines, and where people could come together and connect on a deeper level. We envisioned a community of people who were interested in hearing others' stories and encouraging others. There are thousands and thousands of people who can relate to your struggle. There are so many who have unfulfilling marriages and families that are way out of whack, while their ministry seems to be thriving and growing. What if all of us stood together and said, "NO! We won't sacrifice our family on the altar of ministry or work anymore." What if we lived out God's Word and truly loved those whom God has entrusted to us— our spouses, children, parents—and put them second in our life behind only our relationship with God? What if we didn't put our jobs before our kids? What if we didn't bury our heads in the sand and we actually faced our issues in our relationships and truly trusted God to do the impossible? Is that possible? Yes, it is, but not without support.

That's why we started www.hectictohealthy.com It's a place you can go to share your story, share your journey, and read about other people's journeys. You can encourage others and be encouraged. "When I was with you, you saw the struggles I had, and you hear about the struggles I am having now. You yourselves are having the same kind of struggles" (Phil. 1:30, *NCV*). There is amazing God-given power available when we all come together!

12

ENJOY LIFE

In the end, it's not the years in your life that count. It's the life in your years.

ABRAHAM LINCOLN

It's a Journey, Not a Destination

How do you enjoy life when you are in the middle of difficulty? It's certainly not by looking at your surroundings. It's by looking beyond them. It's a change in scenery and perspective. You view difficulty as an opportunity. You look at what you have, not what has been lost. You see the end as a new beginning. Yes, it's hard, but we have hope. Life isn't a bed of roses unless you plant them for those coming behind you. So why not carry some seed?

Why have we included a chapter on enjoyment in a book about hectic lives? Because, "Weeping may go on all night, but joy comes with the morning" (Ps. 30:5). As we shared with you in the first few chapters, pain was more prevalent than joy for quite a while in our life, but that doesn't mean we were meant to live in it. There is "a time to cry and a time to laugh. A time to grieve and a time to dance" (Eccles. 3:4). One of the wisest people who ever lived said, "So I recommend having fun, because there is nothing better for people to do in this world than to eat, drink, and enjoy life. That way they will experience some happiness along with all the hard work God gives them" (Eccles. 8:15).

Mary and I have found that we need to view a balanced life not so much as a destination, but as a journey. Life balance doesn't have an address; it's more of a road trip. You know you want to go north; you need to go north. You plan and pack to go north, but sometimes life moves you sideways or even south, so you reroute and continue the journey. If we are all on the journey to a balanced life, then why not enjoy the trip?

Anyone who has been on a family vacation understands that traveling is not accident or error free. Occasionally, we all experience engine trouble, a flat tire and accidents along the way. These aren't happy times. They aren't easy times. They are difficult times. We map a route north and we learn from the difficulties we experience along the way, and we keep going. Sure, sometimes we stop or get stopped. Sometimes we even crash, but we assess the damage, get an estimate, get it fixed and start the journey again. Why? Because each day is a new day, and joy comes in the morning.

You may experience a tremendous storm while on your journey, but the sun will come up again. We have never known it not to. You may have stopped from a flat tire, blown engine, or when you see a tornado out your passenger side window. Yes, that's a time to cry, but the irrevocable promise of God comes in the next moment when the tow truck comes by and not only fixes the tire but gives you four new ones! Soon a load of cars on the way to a dealership stops and the driver asks if you need help. Jokingly, you say, yeah, can I trade mine for one of yours, and he says, "Yes, can you wait for a couple of minutes while I unload one?"

You look up in disbelief, your entire family not even looking at you as they have turned away to see the tornado come to a grinding halt when only moments before it had risen ominously above the horizon. We sense the skepticism in your mind. If we hadn't lived it, seen it, tasted it, I would pass it off as biblical truth we haven't experienced yet. We believe it to be true because God's Word tells us it's true, but we just can't give a testimony. We understand the skepticism, but we have experienced the grace, "Now glory be to God! By his mighty power at work within us, he is able to accomplish infinitely more than we would ever dare to ask or hope" (Eph. 3:20).

You may be saying, "Craig and Mary, you don't know what I am going through. What you both described in the first section of this book is magnified and compounded in my life right now. I can't think about joy; it's hard to even fathom tomorrow." We understand. We not only sympathize, but we empathize with you. We wish we could be there in your moment of pain and difficulty to simply give you a hug and let you know that God is faithful.

It's hard to read, "Rejoice in the Lord always. I will say it again: Rejoice!" (Phil. 4:4, *NIV*) when you are in the middle of life's spin. However, the circumstances under which Paul wrote those words were not ideal. In fact, they were awful. Here, Paul is in prison, things are feeling a bit upside down, Paul lets us into his world as he writes these words: "But I am hard-pressed from both directions, having the desire to depart and be with Christ, for that is very much better; yet to remain on in the flesh is more necessary for your sake" (Phil. 1:23-24, *NASB*). Paul is saying that if he could just get away from all this earthly toil and trouble, life would be great. And the only place to experience that amazing life would be with Christ Himself; but he doesn't act on it. He simply makes a statement we all know to be true—that life with Christ would be the absolute best. HOWEVER, that's not what this letter is about. It's not what Paul is about, and it's not what you are about.

It's *all* about living joyfully in the midst of difficulty. Paul says to rejoice in the Lord, not in our circumstances, whether they are good or bad. That's where we find rest and redemption and power instead of pain. Rejoicing isn't an option; and of all people, Paul, who was smack-dab in the middle of difficulty, is telling us to rejoice no matter what. When all other sources of joy are gone, when you are in the pit of despair, it's not the end. It's the beginning, because slowly, gently and with great difficulty, we turn our hearts and minds to the one who created us, to the one who died for us, to the one who has every hair on our head numbered. So, rejoice!

Paul isn't making a suggestion in Philippians 4:4; he is telling us how it's going to be. He is giving us a command. Let me give you an example. When our children were younger, Mary and I would issue commands on a regular basis. Phrases like, "Take out the trash," "Brush your teeth," "Stop hitting your brother" have been voiced repeatedly in our home for several years. These phrases are given with a certain tone and voice. The vocal inflection is direct, implying an exclamation point, not a question mark or period. When a command is given, we expect it to be followed.

It's tough to see a written phrase without seeing the words delivered by the communicator. We miss the nuances that nonverbal clues can give us. How would Paul have delivered the news to us to empower us to rejoice? The great news is, he did. When Paul wrote the words, "Rejoice in the Lord always. I will say it again: Rejoice!" he left us a few grammatical clues. In the Greek language, verbs change form depending on what the subject is and the kind of action indicated. Greek verbs have personality; they have mood and voice; they have a sort of nonverbal quality to them. The word "rejoice" (now hang in there with us for a moment) is in the present active imperative and it's written in the second person, meaning that you and I, the readers, are the ones being spoken to. Paul isn't thinking out loud to himself or speculating on what it would be like to rejoice; he is saying, *you* rejoice.

The present tense of the word "rejoice" tells us when we are to do it. It's giving us a time frame. Do we rejoice now? Later? When the Seahawks win the Super Bowl? Not in this case. No, the present tense of the verb is telling us that the action is continuous and habitual and not based on an event. In other words, we are to continually, habitually rejoice. We are to make rejoicing part of our lifestyle. We are to make it our attitude and outlook on life as we travel through it.

Here is our experience: If God commanded it, He will give the grace, love, mercy and power to follow the command. He is faithful. He gives abundant life, not just a new one. He gives us hope to carry on, and we rejoice; we have joy because of that hope. "Be joyful because you have hope. Be patient when trouble comes, and pray at all times" (Rom. 12:12, *NCV*).

The Art of No

Learning to say no isn't as easy as it seems. Let's face it, some personalities have a hard time saying no. Mary and I are two of them. We aren't talking about saying no to something that is not worthwhile or is unimportant. We are talking about saying no to good things, even great things. How about saying no to an opportunity to feed the homeless? How about saying no to serve on the board of a battered women's shelter? These people, these opportunities, need someone to say yes to them—to help them, serve them, love them. I would like to revise the first sentence in this paragraph: Learning to say no is borderline impossible.

I personally had to learn that when you say yes to some things, you are in essence saying no to other things, and vice versa. Life is like a glass; it has a capacity. Once the capacity is reached, you can no longer put any more into the glass without causing it to overflow. What is more important—sitting at your seven-year-old's soccer practice or feeding the homeless? Should you say yes to your going on a missions trip, or yes to a family vacation?

Learning to say no sounds a whole lot easier to do than it is. The reason this is so tough is that the things we are being asked to do or get involved with are good, worthwhile and often compelling things. If you like saying yes to good, worthwhile and important things, like Mary and I do, you may want to explore the possibility of learning how to say no. The more you say yes, the more it leads to stress; and the more you say no, the more it leads to an acceptable PACE for your season of life.

Jesus knew how to say no. We read about such a time in Mark 5:24. A synagogue leader named Jairus asked Jesus to heal his little daughter who was dying. Jesus left with Jairus, and the crowd followed Him. I like how the *New Living Translation* describes it: "Jesus went with him, and the crowd thronged behind" (Mark 5:24). You get a sense of a large crowd and chaotic environment. When a woman who had been sick for many years came up behind Jesus and touched His robe, she was healed immediately. Jesus realized what had happened, so He turned and asked, "Who touched my clothes?" (v. 30). The disciples were amazed that Jesus knew someone had touched Him or made a reference that someone had touched Him, because He was, no doubt, repeatedly jostled by the crowd as they walked along. It would be hard to know who did the bumping and touching.

Jesus turned to talk to the woman, and during the conversation, the "thronging" crowd still present, messengers came with the painful news:

"While he was still speaking to her, messengers arrived from Jairus's home with the message, 'Your daughter is dead. There's no use troubling the Teacher now' " (v. 35). Jesus was close enough to overhear what was said. I can picture Him leaning in and softly putting His hands on Jairus's cheeks to direct his face to Jesus' eyes. Jairus—shaking, sobbing, broken and bewildered—meets the eyes of Jesus and hears Him say, "Don't be afraid. Just trust me" (v. 36).

Can you picture the moment? The chaos of the crowd; the joy of a woman healed; the pain of the messenger's words; then the moment when Jesus collects Jairus and begins to move in the direction of his house. The crowd and His disciples follow. "Then Jesus stopped the crowd and wouldn't let anyone go with him except Peter and James and John" (v. 37). Jesus said no, you cannot come with me.

Why? Too many people for such a small house? He wanted to teach something to Peter, James and John? He didn't want anyone to see the miracle He was about to perform? We don't know. But we do know that Jesus took the girl's mom and dad, and Peter, James and John, into the room where the little girl was lying (see v. 40). After the miracle, He told them to not tell anyone what had happened. Jesus said yes to three from the crowd that day—Peter, James and John. He said no to the rest. Can we say yes to some and no to the rest? Can we say no to some and yes to the rest?

When someone asks me to do something or volunteer for something, I find myself in a quandary. My natural tendency is to say yes without thinking. I am trying to learn the art of saying no. I say "art" because I don't think it's an exact science. Here's my dilemma. Usually when I am asked to give up my time, I am approached by someone who has all the charisma of a movie star on the big screen and usually represents not only a good cause but also a great one! It's a world-changing idea and vision. I like being around them; I believe in the cause; it's hard to say no.

No isn't always just a two-letter word. You can't just blurt out no when your boss asks you to do something. You may need to expand on it; in fact, we would recommend it. Also, when someone asks you to do something, the phrase "let me pray about it" doesn't count unless you are actually going to pray about it. "Let me pray about it" is the Christian version of no, just in case you were wondering.

Not too long ago, Mary and I were speaking at a conference in New Mexico. After the conference, we were invited to dinner at the home of one of the leaders. There were several people there from the conference, and we had a great time talking, laughing and swapping stories. As the evening was winding down, one of the couples, Kim and Maria, wanted to say a few words. Kim told us that both he and his wife resonated with our story of living life out of its season and experiencing the associated spin and pain that can follow. He shared a bit of their story and how they had experienced difficulty in their relationship with each other. He asked Mary and me to come up, and as we did, he presented us with a painting. Kim is an incredible artist and the painting he gave us is entitled "Starlight." We were overwhelmed at the generosity and power of this gift. It hangs in our office today as a reminder for us of how our life should be lived.

This was not an ordinary painting, but a story told in one act. It was a moment captured in time and released on the canvas. It was a powerful moment as Kim wove the story of the painting's creation. The painted scene is a dad and a mom standing with their child in the middle of a crooked dirt path just outside their home. The story begins in the bottom left-hand side of the canvas and moves up to the half-lit evening sky. Life tends to feel like it's a journey up, doesn't it? Under the soft light of a crescent moon, mom is holding a lantern to illuminate the path, but only where they stand as a family. There are no streetlights. You can't simply point out a direction and say go; you must travel together as a family. Dad is standing next to his wife and son with his hand outstretched, pointing up the crooked path just past the horizon to an old church with a cross atop its steeple.

It is personally symbolic to me. Dad is pointing out that the destination is Christ, but the journey is together. As I look at this picture story, it reminds me of my family's season and, perhaps, how I caused our family to wander off the path or, worse, left them all alone on the path while I explored the side streets looking for what was lost inside me. It reminds me of my and Mary's role and responsibility as parents during this season of our life.

We are here to give direction and point the way. We are here to walk beside our children along the winding road of life until they stand outside their own homes one day with their own families and with an outstretched hand and a lantern providing light and direction for their families.

As I picture me and my family in that scene, I notice something. There are many other homes along the path we are on. Maybe some of them need help. Maybe someone will come out of his home as we walk by and ask for help or offer us something to eat. What will I say? Will we stop?

Will we help? Do I stay and help, and send my family on without me? There are many questions and opportunities along life's journey, and how we answer them, how *you* answer them, is entirely dependent upon the season you are in. I wish we could answer them for you, but we can't.

Here's what we know: You and your family should enjoy your journey together, even when you stumble along the way. There will be skinned knees and hurt feelings, but it's possible to laugh about those things later. If you stop to say yes to everyone on your journey's pathway, you will never get to the destination God has intended for you and your family.

When someone asks you to do something, and you simply do not have the mental, emotional, physical or social time to say yes, or you feel guilty for saying no, paint a picture of your season right now. If you say yes to someone or something, who or what are you saying no to? "Don't be too easily convinced that God really wants you to do all sorts of work you needn't do. Each must do his duty 'in that state of life to which God has called him.' "[1]

Let us plan our way and then trust God for our steps. Let us light our path with His Word and pray for wisdom to learn the *art* of saying no.

The Science of Laughter

It is said that laughter is the best medicine. I'm not sure that scientific research can confirm that laughter is a medicine to treat a severe illness; you can't just laugh away serious pain or difficulty, but there are health benefits to laughter and to having an overall attitude or disposition of cheerfulness.

Research has shown that humor can have pain-killing benefits. In one study, patients who watched funny movies needed less pain medication after orthopedic surgery than did patients who viewed serious movies or no movies at all.[2] Laughing and having a cheerful attitude definitely have some kind of connection to emotional resilience. Laughing at yourself and seeing the humor in situations can take the sting out of defeat and disappointment. We are not saying to laugh and be cheerful in the midst of crisis, but you may be able to laugh about it sometime in the future. Here's an example of what I am talking about.

Let me just blurt it out here and then explain it. Our family was getting ready to go on a trip a few years ago. I was loading up the car with our suitcases, backpacks and pillows. We have an SUV with a hatchback. If you open the back hatch of our SUV, the entire door would swing up from south to north, then stop to be almost parallel to the ground. The door when opened is about five feet ten inches from the ground; I'm over six feet tall. You can guess how this will come into play shortly.

Loading the vehicle is a three-dimensional puzzle to put everyone's stuff in the back and still make room for the people. There is constant loading and unloading to make everything fit. This is a frustrating process, especially for guys, since we think we can always make it fit, no matter what. I started saying things like, "Do we really need to bring all of this? Can't we leave one or two bags here at the house?" Of course no one wants to give up his or her stuff.

After 20 minutes of loading, unpacking, rearranging, repacking, squeezing, pressing, leveraging, adjusting, banging, slamming and so on, one of the kids brings out a carry-on size piece of luggage.

"*What is that?*" You can imagine the tone with which I said it.

"Sorry, Dad, I forgot to bring this out earlier."

Without words, and moving with frustration and anger, I grabbed the bag and flung it around and tried to put the square peg into the round hole, making all sorts of frustrating sounds as I did it. Once it was in, I raised up to give a lecture to all who were listening and, yes, all of them were present. However, when I stood all the way up, my over six-foot-frame met the corner of the five-foot-ten-inch hatch door; the hatch won.

"Excruciating" is the only word I can use to explain the pain that started on the top of my head and like a flash of lightning shot all the way to my feet. I wish I had the spiritual power in that moment to hold my tongue, but I could not. In that moment of sheer pain, I bit it on the way to my knees.

Here's the scene. Dad on his knees—bleeding, probably dying. Kids—all three of them, standing in a row. Completely neutral facial expressions, no doubt praying that Dad would not "lose it" once he regained his equilibrium. Mom standing off to the side, trying to create a bit of space while checking to see if I was okay.

After I spent some time on my knees (it almost sounds spiritual, doesn't it), I looked up and out of the corner of my eye and saw Mary with her hand over her mouth. She wasn't in shock or gasping in horror; she was trying to cover a smirk. I looked at the kids, who were looking at Mom to see if it was okay to express what they were feeling as well.

We all handle these kinds of things in different ways. Alec tries to pucker his lips together to create a vacuum in which to suck the smile off his face. Cameron tries to display genuine concern but with a half-forced frown on his face to offset the smile. I know he wants to write this down as a funny illustration he will use later. "Hey, remember that time when Dad . . ." Karimy, without that filter gene, just laughs.

I know; we are sick people. If the accident doesn't seriously injure you, there is probably going to be a chuckle. In fact, I would say that up to the point of seven stitches or less, you will probably get a laugh. Of course, after a few minutes, I start to laugh too. Yes, in pain, bleeding . . . now we have another story. Somehow it's healing, not to my head but for my heart. Looking at life through a set of optimistic lenses can help us with our resilience in difficult times.

Laughter relieves tension. It motivates and is contagious. Laughter interrupts that fight-or-flight response we all feel from time to time that makes the pulse quicken, breathing grow shallow and adrenaline start rushing through your body. Perpetual stress can trap your body in the fight-or-flight response. Constant stress can weaken your immune system, making you more susceptible to illness. Laughter can actually strengthen your immune system while it lowers your blood pressure. The wisdom of God's Word tells us, "Being cheerful keeps you healthy. It is slow death to be gloomy all the time" (Prov. 17:22, *TEV*). Now how do you feel about that?

Some Proverbial Wisdom

Worry weighs a person down; an encouraging word cheers a person up (Prov. 12:25).

A glad heart makes a happy face; a broken heart crushes the spirit (Prov. 15:13).

Every day is a terrible day for a miserable person, but a cheerful heart has a continual feast (Prov. 15:15, *GOD'S WORD*).

A cheerful look brings joy to the heart, and good news gives health to the bones (Prov. 15:30, *NIV*).

Being cheerful keeps you healthy. It is slow death to be gloomy all the time (Prov. 17:22, *TEV*).

A cheerful heart is good medicine, but a broken spirit saps a person's strength (Prov. 17:22).

SECTION 4

CONTINUING
WALK

13

WATCH OUT

Be careful! Watch out for attacks from the Devil, your great enemy.
He prowls around like a roaring lion, looking for some victim to devour.

1 PETER 5:8

It's the Prowl, Not the Roar

I have heard several sermons on this particular verse, as well as several sermons where this particular verse was used. For some reason, my mind always paints the same picture: a very large, very aggressive and very dangerous animal—a predator who is at the apex of the food chain. I focus on *what* the lion looks like, entirely forgetting about his tactics. While having the picture of an aggressive animal that wants to devour you is helpful in avoiding him, it's also helpful to get a clear understanding of how the lion hunts; you need to know his tactics.

While we don't have a lion at our house, we do have a cat. Yes, it's a far cry from a lion, but I have noticed some similarities. While Mary and I were sitting in the backyard, our cat was outside exploring. A few birds landed in the yard not too far away and caught his attention. Oddly enough, he didn't burst off running. He immediately crouched low to the ground and froze just like a small cat mannequin. It was almost as if he were trying to appear invisible. I must tell you that our cat has uncanny speed. As a kitten he would move so fast we named him Turbo. Even with his lightning-fast speed, his first response was to crouch, freeze, wait and then slowly and methodically start to move. The movement was undetectable to the prey. It took him several minutes to go a few feet. He moved slowly and deliberately, completely stopping occasionally when he felt the birds had sensed his presence. There was no twitch in his muscles and he exhibited laser-like focus. He moved as if he were mechanical.

The birds didn't know he was there. Turbo got within a few feet of his prey—you could see him begin to coil up all his energy into his hind legs. He was getting ready to uncoil all that power into a massive attack. All at once that energy was uncoiled in an explosion like a bullet shot out of a gun. *Mary* jumped up to scare the birds away. Now, that's *one* of the ways our enemy attacks. He stalks, watches and then pounces. It's the prowl, not the roar. It's intentionally subtle. Our enemy wants us to feel a false sense of security and remain unaware that we are being hunted.

In C. S. Lewis's classic work *The Screwtape Letters*, he records the correspondence between two imaginary demons. The uncle and mentor, Screwtape, is writing to his nephew, a junior-level demon named Wormwood. Screwtape is giving advice on how to tempt and topple the Christian to whom he has been assigned. In letter number three, Screwtape gives the following advice to Wormwood: "Aggravate that most useful human characteristic, the horror and neglect of the obvious."[1] The subtle neglect of the obvious. How does that transform our thinking today?

I never paid too much attention to all that spiritual warfare stuff. I knew enough about the devil to stay away from the topic. I had heard the "spiritual armor" talk of Ephesians 6 several times—from a felt board to multimedia to drama and back again, but I never really understood it until I was forced to deal with it. Spiritual warfare seemed far less scary to me when we talk about the shield of faith and helmet of salvation. It's quite another thing when you read about demonic oppression and possession or see a movie that depicts such things. We need to understand that our enemy is not a little red cartoon guy running around with horns and a pitchfork. He is active. He is on the prowl, looking to destroy and devour.

Go ahead, ask the question: "Craig, why do you have a chapter on spiritual warfare in a book that is talking about burnout and balance?" Well, for me, it was directly connected to the speed of my life and the desire to do more. Let me reiterate what we talked about in section one. The faster life moves, the more you miss. Your life may feel like a smooth round stone that has just been skipped across a smooth glassy lake. Skip, skip, skip, skip it goes, but no matter how hard that rock has been thrown, it eventually stops . . . and sinks. There is never another outcome. You get more productivity out of some stones, depending on the speed and structure, but they always sink.

We should also emphasize the final words in 1 Peter 5:8. The verse says, "looking for some victim to devour." Our enemy isn't waiting for you to be in crisis before he attacks you. He is looking for you. Our enemy is not passive; he is active. He is searching, seeking to devour us.

We have already talked about our enemy stalking in stealth. Although he prowls, he is likened to a lion. He will pursue you with all the animosity of a hungry predator. Think of the documentaries on the wilds of Africa, as Mary already mentioned in chapter 11. The lion waits for one of the herd to get isolated from the rest and he attacks the one who is most tired, most defenseless, or most unaware.

The subtle temptations our enemy offers are simply traps to gain greater control of our lives. If we succumb to the smallest of temptations, we allow his influence. If we keep giving in, he gains more control. He starts with influence, then control and, finally, to ownership. While I don't believe a true Christ-follower can be demonically possessed, I do believe you can be controlled, and I do believe there are different levels of control.

I had to learn that with the devil, "Every day is war." God's Word says, "For we are not fighting against people made of flesh and blood, but against the evil rulers and authorities of the unseen world, against those mighty powers of darkness who rule this world, and against wicked spirits in the heavenly realms" (Eph. 6:12). There is a powerful unseen world that is unleashing all its resources against us. I wish we could absorb this concept of what's going on around us and really understand what's at stake every minute of every day.

Forgive to Live

One of the ways our enemy leverages his way into our life is through our inability to forgive others. I (Craig) was forced to deal with a strong enemy attack in my life that was largely brought about by my inability to forgive people in my past. I held on to feelings of hurt, resentment and bitterness to such an extent that I gave the devil an opportunity, or foothold, in my life. I gave him an entry point of access that he could exploit.

When I say "forced to deal with it," I literally mean *forced*. For several years, I fought with night terrors. Not nightmares, night terrors. Dreams that were so vivid I would feel like I was being physically held down in my bed. Several times, Mary would wake up to see me in a virtual struggle. She would try to wake me up in the middle of my panic as I tried to fight my way out of the event. This would happen a few times a month and usually around a time when ministry was going very well. I would blame these terrors on our enemy's attack of someone who was making a difference, who was investing in others. I took the "bring it on" attitude, or even the "if you want to fight, let's do it" attitude. This was not the right way to "put on all of God's armor so that you will be able to stand firm against all strategies and tricks of the Devil" (Eph. 6:11).

Those times when we become angry at someone and then let that anger simmer and settle deep into our hearts is when we have given our enemy an opportunity. Paul writes in Ephesians 4:26-27: "And 'don't sin by letting anger gain control over you.' Don't let the sun go down while you are still angry, for anger gives a mighty foothold to the Devil." What is a foothold exactly? A foothold is any spot you can find to get a more secure grip.

A few years ago, I took a crash course in rock climbing while filming a curriculum series in Joshua Tree National Park. I was not aware of the strength, agility and keen awareness you need to rock climb. I found myself looking around me in all directions, trying to figure out where to step (or *try* to step) next. Navigating up the side of a huge rock is like putting together a puzzle without looking at the box-top picture. What you are constantly looking for is the next foothold where you can put your foot in order to leverage your next move or your next position. This isn't a fast process. Sometimes when I had a good grip and hold that was supporting most of my weight, I would pause and rest. I would get a better look at the rock and plan out my next three of four moves. Sometimes I would have to move left to right in order to move up. It's slow going. I would use every muscle in my body to creep along at a snail's pace, just to move 10 inches. If I could find a spot in the rock where there was a crack or break, I would head for it. If I could get a foot on or in a little ledge, it gave me a firm position to take the next step.

That's what our enemy does as he tries to climb onto and into our lives. He looks for a position that will give his evil forces what they need to advance. When we harbor anger, resentment, bitterness and an unwillingness to forgive others, the devil has found a great spot to not only stand but also to advance and progress deeper.

I honestly didn't know the ramifications of allowing my anger to get control over me. I didn't know that it gave the devil an opportunity for control in my life. My inability to forgive became a habit, and it would go something like this. I would get angry at someone I felt had offended me. I would not address the anger or bitterness I felt. I would not forgive. Over time, the feeling of upset, hurt or even hate would go away. In effect, I would "Let the sun go down on my anger." I would fail to forgive and end up angry and resentful. I would rationalize my anger to appease my feelings. There were several people—including myself—that I needed to forgive. Some were people I could not even remember until I asked God for help. In my case, you could add ledge upon ledge where the enemy could get a foothold and further advance his position in my life. I believe the night terrors I experienced up until five years ago were linked in a very specific way to this issue of unforgiveness in my life.

God had to get my attention in a powerful way to get me to address it. Have you ever had God get your attention? I mean, really get your attention? Not the subtle promptings or leadings through a sermon or service, but a thunderous event that jolts you out of your skin? God taught me a valuable lesson through a series of events that would rival the handwriting on the wall of Daniel 5, or a verbal shout from heaven above. He encountered me in such a way that I knew I needed to act.

I was meeting with a couple of guys weekly and reading through the book *The Bondage Breaker* by Neil Anderson. Dr. Anderson was a professor of mine at Biola University. His work on the topic of spiritual warfare is well documented and his lectures and books have helped thousands of people, including me, understand our battle against our enemy and the power that Christ has in our life. I was about an hour early to our weekly meeting and decided to stop at a nearby fast-food establishment for a beverage. After sitting down at a booth with the three books I had brought with me, I started thumbing through the pages with all the vigor my ADD could afford me. I was randomly picking up books, glancing through the pages to see what would jump out at me.

I stopped to get up for a refill and turned the book over and placed it on the table upside down at the page where I had stopped. When I came back, I picked up *The Bondage Breaker* and started to read where I had left off. I started just below the middle of the page. The bold-faced type began with the words, "Don't wait until you feel like forgiving. You will never get there. Once you choose to forgive, Satan will have lost his power over you in that area."[2] I thought to myself, *That makes sense.* Maybe in some small way I needed to do a better job of forgiving those around me. Upon brief reflection, I could think of a few people I needed to forgive. Perhaps some bitterness was lingering in my heart. Maybe my night terrors were connected to my lack of forgiveness. Had I been too busy to forgive? Had I suppressed it? Not cared enough about it? I wasn't too sure, but I highlighted the quote and picked up another book.

The quote was good enough to highlight but not necessarily good enough to act on. Sometimes when I am reading a book I will highlight a quote or even make a note but never return to it. I'm not sure why that is, but it's a frequent process for me as I read. Nevertheless, I moved on to the next book I brought with me.

An hour later, I connected with the guys for our meeting. As the meeting was wrapping up, Ed said, "Oh, wait a minute. I was looking through some stuff this week and came across something you may want." The title on the front was *Steps to Freedom in Christ, Youth Edition.* I was obviously well past my youth chronologically, but apparently not spiritually. I gave the customary "thanks" and thumbed through the pages as I walked away. Then it hit me. Right in the middle of the hall, and right in the middle of page 8 there was a quote: "Don't wait until you feel like forgiving. You will never get there. Once you choose to forgive, Satan will have lost his power over you in that area."

What? Are you kidding me? I just read that quote an hour ago. Could it be that God was trying to get my attention? It was a little weird to see the same quote in two different publications, both within an hour or two of each other. I walked out to the car with Anderson's quote swirling around in my mind. Once I got in the car, I called Mary. She asked how the study went and I told her it went great, and then I told her about this uncanny coincidence with the quotes. I didn't tell her what the quote was or what the topic was. I just told her that I had read a quote before the meeting and then the same quote was brought up again as I was leaving the meeting.

I asked her what she was doing. She said she was reading Stasi Eldredge's book *Captivating*, and she had just read something amazing. Before I knew it, she had put down the phone to go get the book. Immediately, my head was aware of what my heart felt. I knew what the quote was before she got back to the phone. She returned, saying, "Listen to this great line. She is quoting some guy named Anderson: 'Don't wait to forgive until you feel like forgiving. You will never get there.'" I'm not sure what she said after that.

Right there in the car, I broke down crying, sobbing, emotionally broken and spiritually bankrupt. *Forgiveness.* This was the problem and the answer in one quote. I can't remember another time in my life when God was so relentlessly pursuing me on an issue to bring about full resolve. The same quote, on the same topic, in less than three hours, from three different sources. *Yes, God. You have my attention.*

Revelation was the first step for me. The next was participation. I had to sit down and write out the names of people I could remember not forgiving, even those I was angry with or bitter about. Forgiveness isn't easy. At least it wasn't for me. I made a list of past hurts and people I had not forgiven that went all the way back to when I was eight years old. One by one, in front of my prayer partners, I read the list out loud to God, saying their name and what I forgave them for. To be honest, I didn't want to say a few of the names. I clenched my teeth and, with an almost regretful spirit, I said those names and what I forgave them for. Small things, big things, all things and everything I could remember. Honestly, my feelings didn't follow my actions, but my freedom did.

I now understand on a deeper level why we *have* to forgive others. If we don't forgive others, it allows the enemy to get leverage from which to further advance into our lives. We give him access to our life when we allow anger to steep into bitterness and an unforgiving attitude. Our enemy uses this against us to take advantage of us, to influence us, to oppress us.

The night terrors I was experiencing vanished immediately. I can tell you from the moment of my encounter with forgiveness up until the writing of this paragraph, I have only experienced two night terrors, and they were different. I knew how to pray out loud; I knew how to hand it over to Jesus and His angels and go back to sleep in peace.

As I look back, I realize that as my life started to spin I was less willing to forgive. I became less flexible and more controlling, less aware of others' needs and more aware of my own. This led to pride and the soft whispers of the enemy saying, "You don't have to take that. You don't deserve that. Who are they to talk to you that way? It's their fault, not yours." Soon bitterness came knocking and unforgiveness answered the door. In walked the enemy, immediately looking for the next place to put his feet. God got my attention. Maybe He is trying to get yours too?

It's in Your Job Description

When it comes to forgiveness, I can't help but think of Job. He was the poster child for forgiveness, patience and grace. His entire situation was filled with one painful event after another; and to make matters worse, his friends were intent on pointing fingers of blame at him for his current situation. I'm sure that I wouldn't have fared as well as Job did, given his situation.

Job is well known for his incredible persistence in the midst of pain. If we look deeper into his story, God's blessing upon his life is evident after he made a choice to forgive and pray for those who called themselves friends, yet had caused Job an incredible amount of suffering through their hurtful words and accusations.

Job's story starts on the battlefield of spiritual war. We read in Job 1:6-20 and 2:1-7 that the Lord permitted Satan to test Job, to do whatever he wanted with Job's possessions, even permitting him to cause bodily pain. Job felt the immediate pressure of the attack by losing servants and livestock, then sons and daughters, then feeling the pain of a physical ailment. Yet even after these calamities, Job falls to the ground and worships (see Job 1:20).

For many of us, multiple calamities would be the end. But Job, crushed with discouragement and thrown into the middle of despair, hangs in there. Then his friends show up. "When Job's three friends, Eliphaz the Temanite, Bildad the Shuhite and Zophar the Naamathite, heard about all the troubles that had come upon him, they set out from their homes and met together by agreement to go and sympathize with him and comfort him" (Job 2:11, *NIV*).

Job's three friends may have started out with good intentions, but they soon resorted to allegations and accusations. Job's friends moved from extending a hand to pointing a finger. Eliphaz said to Job, "You are supposed to be a wise man, and yet you give us all this foolish talk. You are nothing but a windbag . . . Have you no fear of God, no reverence for him? Your sins are telling your mouth what to say. Your words are based on clever deception. But why should I condemn you? Your own mouth does!" (Job 15:2,4-6). This was probably not the sympathy and comfort Job was looking for.

The good intentions of three friends, at some point, went sideways. The ones Job thought he could rely on in the midst of pain were now crisis contributors. If you listen carefully, you can hear the emotion in Job's voice as he responds, "I have heard all this before. What miserable comforters you are! . . . I could say the same things if you were in my place. I could spout off my criticisms against you and shake my head at you. But that's not what I would do. I would speak in a way that helps you. I would try to take away your grief" (Job 16:2,4-5).

Job was physically broken, mentally exhausted, emotionally depleted and now relationally attacked. How was he able to stay honest before the Lord? How was he able to keep his integrity intact? I would imagine it was his heart of worship and proper soul care.

Eliphaz continued, "Is it because of your reverence for him that he accuses and judges you [Job]? Not at all! It is because of your wickedness! Your guilt has no limit!" (Job 22:4-5).

Job had the right perspective and the nature of God hidden deep in his soul. "Large God equals small problems" could have been his motto. "If only I knew where to find God, I would go to his throne and talk with him there. . . . But he knows where I am going. . . . So he will do for me all he has planned. He controls my destiny" (Job 23:3,10,14).

Even though Job was searching, he knew he had been found. Isn't that the way we are at times? In the midst of difficulty and uncertainty we still know God is there. As I read through Job, I hear a man who questions but has answers, a man of weakness yet great power, one who wants to give up but has a spiritual tenacity worthy of an award. Maybe we could call it being authentic or being real.

I have been in places spiritually where I knew God was in control, yet I questioned my own direction. Even though life is uncertain at times, when we have spun out of control and are lying in a heaped-up pile of rags on the side of the road, we can still be certain of a God who never changes; a God who is in control; a God who is intimately involved with our life. Pain may come as a result of choices we have made, or God simply allows pain into our lives. The difficulty, as Job experienced, was that while he was down, his friends were no help. It sounds like it would have been a minor comfort for Job if they simply weren't there. Perhaps no friends at this time would have been better than bitter friends.

Job endured much pain at the hands of his three friends, but the most difficult part was still ahead. It's about forgiveness. In Job's story, forgiveness was the key, and God's blessing was the lock. In Job's case, when he inserted the key, the lock opened.

The Lord had a conversation with Job and his three friends. "I am angry with you and your two friends, because you have not spoken of me what is right, as my servant Job has. . . . Sacrifice a burnt offering for yourselves. My servant Job will pray for you." After Job had prayed for his friends, the LORD made him prosperous again and gave him twice as much as he had before. . . . The LORD blessed the latter part of Job's life more than the first" (Job 42:7,8,10,12, *NIV*).

It's hard for me to forgive even the small things under normal circumstances. By normal, I mean life is moving along, someone offends me, I forgive them, life continues to move along. We would agree that Job's situation had a bit more intensity to it. Under the pressure of the death of family members, the loss of his wealth, and excruciating and ongoing physical pain, he had these three guys telling him the reason he was experiencing these things was because he was arrogant, full of pride and was hiding his sin.

If forgiveness was the key, I might have thrown it away. Job does not throw it away, and he goes one further: he prays for his friends. Job 42:10 recounts the cause and effect of Job's prayer: "*After* Job had prayed for his friends, the LORD made him prosperous again and gave him twice as much as he had before" (*NIV*, emphasis added). Job's life was restored *after* he prayed for his friends, not before. Job's life was not restored *until* he prayed for his friends. "He who can pray for another cannot entertain enmity against him."[3]

Would God have blessed Job if he had not prayed for his friends? I don't think so, simply because the Lord waited to restore and bless Job until after he prayed. As a result, God then blessed him. God even doubled Job's blessing: "The LORD blessed the latter part of Job's life more than the first" (Job 42:12, *NIV*).

I hope these words are encouraging to you. You may be reading these words saying, "I am at the mid-point of my life, or even past it. I have been in SPIN for many years. In fact, my kids are in college. I cannot go back, I cannot get a re-do with my family or my children."

Listen, just because you have made mistakes in the past doesn't mean you can't get on track in the future. Yes, our enemy will do everything in his power to pull you back to whisper into your ear, "Some mistakes you will never stop paying for," but it's not true. Go back and ask for forgiveness of those you feel you have offended. It may be the key to God's blessing in your life. Forgiveness isn't just to keep our enemy out but to keep God's blessing in. "Job's troubles began in Satan's malice, which God restrained; Job's restoration began in God's mercy, which Satan could not oppose."[4]

If you were to create a position description for Christ-followers, you might include several things like kindness, goodness and gentleness. Yet, it's forgiveness that resonates deep in our hearts when we forgive a wrong that has been committed against us. I have felt this forgiveness in my life on a personal level and on a spiritual level. The interesting thing is, once you have been forgiven of something great, it's hard not to extend that forgiveness to someone else. Of all the things we could or should be, *forgiving* tops the list. You could even say that it's part of our *Job* description.

14

ANSWER HIM

God's goodness is spurred by His nature, not by our worthiness.

MAX LUCADO

What Do You Want Me to Do for You?

Have you ever had someone say to you, "Hey, what do you want me to do for you today?" And mean it? Maybe you have a flat tire on the side of the road and a neighborly person pulls up alongside you and asks, "Can I do something for you today?" What if you were on a coffee run for the office and you had two full trays of Grande Caramel somethings, and as you approached the door someone asks you, "Can I help you today?" How you answer these questions could influence the rest of your day, week or, in the case of Bartimaeus, your life.

However, it's not just *how* you answer the question; it's *who* is offering to help. Does the person have the power or resources to fulfill your request? Can that person make what you are asking for a reality? Bartimaeus wasn't asking for something as trivial as help with opening a door. He was asking for his sight to be restored. He was asking for a miracle.

We know a little bit about blindness in our family, from both the physical realm and the spiritual realm. Our son Cameron, who was born with healthy eyesight, experienced a tragic injury at the age of three that caused blindness in his right eye. He went from seeing to blindness, in an instant. I can remember that day at the hospital as I almost ran into the doctor coming out of the operating room. With his mask still on his face, he spoke to Mary and me. He repeated what his eyes had already said, "I'm sorry, your son is going to be blind . . ." I didn't hear anything after that. I can't describe the rush of emotion I felt as those words bounced around in my head.

Cameron sustained a severe eye injury. The initial surgery took three hours and 18 stitches across his cornea just to close the wound. As we sat down with the doctor, he sketched on a napkin and tried to explain the intricacies of the eye and the extent of the injury. I eventually asked, "What is the best we can hope for?" He replied, "Well, I hope we can save the eye and maybe he will be able to see light and dark. If he can see light and dark, that means the retina is attached and there may be a long-shot chance that he could see shapes, with corrected vision, but that's about it. If you try to rehabilitate the eye, you are looking at nine surgeries, at the least. It's going to be a long haul. Or you can just remove the eyeball and replace it with a glass eye. He's young enough that it may even track with the other eye."

What do you say to that? How do you respond?

To date, Cameron has had 14 surgeries, including a cornea transplant, lens implant and surgeries to correct the position of his eye. Six months after the injury and several surgeries, the doctor required us to patch his good eye in an attempt to force his injured eye to start working again. Watching Cameron walk around the house with his tiny Thomas the Tank Engine umbrella, instinctively using it as a walking stick, and not understanding why it had to be this way was emotionally gut-wrenching.

I can imagine, on a very small scale, what Bartimaeus must have felt like. Luke 18:35-43 tells his story. We know Bartimaeus used to be able to see, but sometime in his life, he became blind. Whatever viable form of work he used to do, he could do no more. Life changed for him. He would sit at the gates to the city and beg for a handout. That was all he could do. His life was now conditional upon the grace and mercy of others. Until . . . Jesus came by and extended His grace and mercy, which remained with Bartimaeus for the rest of his life.

I can't help but look at this story and draw some parallels between physical sight and spiritual sight. I'm sure many of us have started out life with good intentions, noble causes or even a desire to make a difference. I know I did, but somewhere along the journey I neglected the important things in favor of the easy things, and then things became a little blurry.

You once had perfect spiritual vision to read and pass life's tests with no problem, but you haven't been to the Doctor lately and you are losing your sight. Even if you have lost all of your spiritual sight, there is help and hope from this point forward.

As Bartimaeus sat begging on the side of the road, he could hear the crowd coming. After all, he had sat at that gate for a long time, day in and day out. He knew the sounds, he knew the voices, but this was different. It piqued his curiosity. He knew the crowd coming into the city was not an ordinary crowd. Maybe he could hear the pushing, the shoving, the fervor of the group. He didn't know what all the commotion was about, but he did know it was coming his way. He asked a bystander what was going on and he learned that Jesus was passing by. Bartimaeus didn't go back to begging; he started shouting! "Then the blind man shouted, 'Jesus, Son of David, have mercy on me!' The people at the front of the crowd told the blind man to be quiet. But he shouted even louder, 'Son of David, have mercy on me!' " (Luke 18:38-39, GOD'S WORD). Bartimaeus wasn't about to let an opportunity for healing pass him by. He didn't care what the crowd thought about him. He got louder as the crowd got closer.

A poor blind beggar's life was about to be changed. However, I don't think his life would have been changed if he had gone with the crowd's instructions. The crowd told him to be quiet. I can hear one of those in the crowd saying, "Don't bother Jesus. Sit down and be quiet." Bartimaeus only got louder. In fact, he was loud enough to get the attention of at least some of the people at the front of the crowd. The crowd must have been coming toward him. This is important to me, because of what happens next. Jesus stopped. He didn't keep walking toward Bartimaeus; He stopped short of Bartimaeus. Next He told those in the crowd to bring Bartimaeus to Him. I love how Mark records this part of the story: "The blind man [Bartimaeus] threw off his coat, jumped up, and went to Jesus" (Mark 10:50, *GOD'S WORD*).

I wonder how many times I continued to beg God for things when the reality was that it was going to take a little work on my part. As life started to SPIN for me and as my spiritual eyesight was growing weak, maybe I should have just gotten up and run to Him—thrown off my coat of pride and arrogance and run toward the voice I knew to be true and right. What would have happened if Bartimaeus had just sat there? What if he hadn't moved *toward* Jesus? Would Jesus have moved toward him? Would Bartimaeus have been healed? I don't know. I am reasonably sure that we cannot expect God to do what we won't do.

I am not talking about works for salvation or works in order to get God's blessing. To obey is better than sacrifice (see 1 Sam. 15:22), but I am talking about doing the self-discovery and soul care that is necessary to regain your sight.

We prayed and fasted for Cameron. We asked for a miracle over and over, and we went ahead and had all the surgeries that were required. Why did we have the surgeries? Couldn't God simply heal Cameron—water into wine, walking on water kinds of stuff? The answer is yes. However, we chose to move *toward* Christ's healing power and not sit and beg.

Cameron's eyesight got better over time. His corrected vision stopped at 20/400. You are considered legally blind when your vision is 20/200. He could see light and dark, blurred shapes and colors, but that was about it. We used to play a game with him and hold up his different stuffed animals to see if he could tell the difference between Micky Mouse, Mama Kitty and a teddy bear. Mary and I had continually asked God for Cameron to see 20/20 in that injured eye. A miracle for sure. We had not shared that part of our prayer (the 20/20 part) with anyone except God.

I finished speaking at a conference in Toronto, Canada, and walked to the back of the auditorium to call Mary. The conference was wrapping up. The host was saying a few final words and was just about to pray when a lady walked up on stage. She asked if she could say a few words, then went on to say that she and her husband wanted to pray for Cameron and our family.

I was hoping the host would dismiss the request in a polite and gracious manner by simply acknowledging the request, praying and thanking everyone for coming. He didn't. "I think that's a good idea," he responded. "Can we get Craig back up here on the stage? We would like to pray for his family and Cameron's healing." I felt shocked, embarrassed and a little hesitant to walk back up to the stage.

My attitude was poor and my faith was weak. I didn't want to get up. I didn't want to move *toward* Jesus. I'm sorry to say that it was the pressure of the audience that moved me forward. Perhaps not unlike Bartimaeus, I needed some help since I wasn't seeing clearly. I told Mary I would call her back and hung up the phone. I walked to the front and stood on stage with the host and the lady who wanted to pray. We bowed our heads and she started to pray.

It was a different kind of prayer. The prayer was intensely conversational; she was searching for the next words to say. It was like she was actually talking to someone. She would pause after a request as if she expected God to answer verbally. I was cynical as I stood there on the platform, but I maintained my outward awareness by looking like I should look, with my head bowed and hands clasped together in front of me.

During a long pause in the prayer, the Holy Spirit got my attention. The lady who was praying for Cameron was searching for her words but couldn't find them. "And Lord we pray for Cameron's healing and we pray . . ." and then the pause. It felt as if the person she was having the conversation with hadn't finished talking, so she was waiting. She wasn't stuck; she was listening. She continued with the prayer, ". . . we pray for 20/20 vision."

Was that coincidence? Mary and I had talked and prayed specifically for 20/20 vision and had not told anyone about it. Here I was, thousands of miles away from home, with people I didn't know. I wasn't sure what to think about what I'd just heard. She continued, "If there is anyone here who believes this is possible, please stand and stretch out your hand as a symbol of agreement with this prayer." I looked up to see 500 people standing with their hands outstretched toward me. It was a powerful and defining moment in my journey. I knew God had touched Cameron's life in that moment.

I called Mary to tell her what had happened, and I was anxious for the next doctor's visit when I knew Cameron would see 20/20. A few months later, we went to see his eye doctor. Cameron read the chart at his usual 20/400. There was no healing, no 20/20 vision. We wondered, *Now what? God, You gave us a promise. We are trusting You. Believing You.*

You keep moving toward Jesus, not away from Him. Bartimaeus did just that. There he was, standing in front of Jesus. The formerly loud and rambunctious crowd waited in silence. Jesus asked, "What do you want me to do for you?" The blind man said, "Lord, I want to see" (Luke 18:41, *NIV*). I can guess at a conversation in the back of the crowd: "What happened? Did Jesus heal him? Did He heal that guy? What happened?" "No." "What happened then?" "Jesus asked him a question." "A question? Does He know that guy is blind?"

Why didn't Jesus just heal Bartimaeus where he was? I think Jesus wanted him to move from where he was to where He wanted him to be, which was closer to Him. He wanted Bartimaeus to make an attempt. I'm sure it was more comfortable for Bartimaeus to stay where he was. Walking through a crowd when you are blind cannot be the easiest thing to do. It's the same with us. Moving toward Jesus is not without hindrances. Bartimaeus even threw aside his outer coat as he made his way to Jesus. Sometimes we need to leave behind things that could cause us to trip and fall on our way to Him. What do we need to get rid of to keep us moving in the right direction? Once you are there in His presence, face to face, answer Him. Bartimaeus knew what to say: "Lord, I want to see." And he did.

Our heavenly Father is asking each of us the same question: "What do you want me to do for you?" Maybe your answer is, "God, I want You to save my family," or "God, I want You to help me conquer my fears. God, I want You to restore my marriage. God, I want You to restore my spiritual vision. God, I want my son to see 20/20."

We arrived at our appointment at 4:00 PM. We had decided to get a second opinion regarding Cameron's vision and were visiting a new doctor that had been recommended by a co-worker. Cameron sat in the doctor's chair and completed the same eye tests that he had taken many times before. Nothing was out of the ordinary until . . . until the doctor changed a few settings on the machine, and Cameron read the 20/200 line. From there, he moved on to read the 20/100 line, then 20/80, then 20/40. Tears streamed down our faces as we watched our miracle unfold before our eyes. Cameron was blind, but now he could see.

Bartimaeus regained his sight immediately—an instant miracle. Cameron received his sight over time, just like the blind man in Mark 8:22-25, whose sight was restored in steps. We can regain our spiritual sight. For some it may be immediate, and for others it will take some time, but clarity will come. Keep moving toward Jesus, and when the question comes, "What do you want Me to do for you?" by all means, answer Him honestly and with the faith of a child.

"So let us come boldly to the throne of our gracious God. There we will receive his mercy, and we will find grace to help us when we need it" (Heb. 4:16).

All the King's Horses and All the King's Men

Occasionally, people would ask Cameron what happened to his eye. "I broke it," was his response as a three-year-old. Broken is a concept we all understand. If something isn't working properly, it's broken. That language is true for electronics and people alike. Where they differ is their replacement value. You replace the remote because it's cheaper than fixing it. Toss the broken one and buy a new one. It's okay to do this with a remote, but not people. God doesn't do this with us. He restores; He never replaces.

In times of trouble, God is with us, and when we are knocked down, we get up again (2 Cor. 4:9, *CEV*).

We all love nursery rhymes. We learned them as children and recite them to our own kids as they grow up. When I was a child, I can't ever remember asking my mom the meaning of "Hickory Dickory Dock," "Jack and Jill" or "Humpty Dumpty." I took them all at face value. Yes, the mouse ran up the clock; yes, Jack did fall down and break his crown, and of course all the king's horses and all the king's men couldn't put Humpty together again.

History tells us that Humpty Dumpty was an egg-shaped character in a Mother Goose nursery rhyme. He fell off a wall and got broken. If you take this nursery rhyme at face value, you can bet that poor old Humpty Dumpty is broken beyond repair. He certainly can't be fixed. All the king's horses and all the king's men couldn't even put him back together again.

Where did this Humpty Dumpty guy come from? The history of nursery rhymes can be vague and subject to urban legend passed down from generation to generation. Humpty Dumpty is no exception. Depending on who or what you read, you will find several assumptions about our dear Humpty Dumpty. Some say that he was a real person; others say he was a cannon. (Yes, a cannon, the kind that shoots cannonballs.) Some claim it was a beverage consumed at a pub. Some claim he was, of all things, an egg. The first publication of the nursery rhyme was in 1810.

> Humpty Dumpty sat on a wall,
> Humpty Dumpty had a great fall;
> Threescore men and threescore more,
> Cannot place Humpty Dumpty as he was before.[1]

The language of the nursery rhyme has changed over time. The Old English was replaced with new words. You may have seen or heard it like this:

> Humpty Dumpty sat on a wall;
> Humpty Dumpty had a great fall.
> All the King's horses
> And all the King's men
> Couldn't put Humpty together again![2]

"Okay, Craig, seriously? Enough of the nursery rhymes. What's your point?" Here's the point. Humpty Dumpty *can* be put back together again. What started out as a nursery rhyme to amuse and teach little children in the 1800s, now is a cultural reminder that when we fall and break, we simply cannot be put back together again. Something that started out as an innocent rhyme subtly changed over the years. Leave it up to our enemy to slowly twist and turn good things into bad, a rhyme into an unhealthy reminder for broken people.

Are you now saying, "Craig, you are really overthinking this nursery rhyme thing"? Okay, I hear you. I am not saying the nursery rhyme is wrong. In fact I don't believe all the king's horses and all the king's men could put Humpty together again, but perhaps a Carpenter could.

What if you are a modern version of that Humpty Dumpty character? You may have been sitting on a wall of pride, a wall of arrogance, a wall of impurity, a wall of indiscretion, a wall of lies and, yes, depending on how long you were up there adding bricks, you either had a short fall or a long one. Maybe you were up on that wall for a long time. You had a lot of time to build, time to add scaffolding and reinforce it all with metal beams. Depending on where you were in your process when you fell, the fall stunned, splintered or shattered you. A 3-foot fall hurts; a 30-foot fall harms and a 300-foot fall hemorrhages. But no matter what, Jesus heals.

You may feel hurt or harmed, or maybe you are hemorrhaging. God cares. He knows, and He can put you back together. You won't look the same—Humpty never did. People see the cracks; they see the evidence of the brokenness. Every time Humpty looked in the mirror, he saw scars and brokenness, pieces that reminded him of a lengthy fall. I'm sure that when he looks in the mirror he thinks, *What if . . . ? What if I hadn't slipped? What if I hadn't taken that spill off the wall or what if . . . ? What if I was pushed?*

You may think pointing the finger at someone else may be a way to heal the brokenness. It's not. There is a rumor, although not forensically proven, that Mr. Dumpty's fall wasn't accidental. Let me put all rumors to rest. He wasn't pushed. He fell because he was off balance. He wasn't pushed and he didn't jump. He fell. He wasn't cracked; he was broken.

Some would say he was broken beyond repair, but it's not true. It is true that all the king's horses and all the king's men couldn't put Humpty back together again. That's why God sent His only Son for just such an occasion. He didn't send Jesus for the Humpty on the wall but the Humpty after the fall. He was sent to fix, mend, redeem, buy back and offer a second chance. He was sent to raise up, bring new life, speak a new word, heal, empower and protect. He was sent to extend grace, empathy and compassion. He wasn't sent to catch Humpty Dumpty, but to pick up the pieces after he fell. He came to bring hope to each of our broken lives—to cracked hearts and broken spirits. Jesus came to bring hope and to tell Mr. Dumpty that the ground is not the end of his journey; it's the beginning of a new one.

"Wait a minute, Craig! The ground *is* the end. Have you lost your paradoxical mind?" Exactly! The definition of a paradox is "a statement or proposition that seems self-contradictory or absurd but in reality expresses a possible truth."[3] We get the word "paradox" from two words "para," meaning "contrary," and "doxa," meaning "opinion." So a paradox is a contrary opinion; it's illogical and sometimes absurd. On the other hand, a paradox is logical, valid and truthful. Even the definition of "paradox" is a paradox. The Bible is full of paradox. Paul used it in 2 Corinthians 12:10 when he said, "For when I am weak, then I am strong." And Jesus used paradox when He said, "many who are first will be last" in Matthew 19:30 (*NIV*). Although I am not in the same company, I would like to submit a paradox to you. The ground is a paradox. That cold, hard, unforgiving ground that Humpty Dumpty was hurling toward is not the end, but a new beginning if you believe in paradox.

Just as the words to this rhyme have changed over time, so have the meanings based on time and culture. Each generation will bring its own nuances and beliefs and will impress them on their version of this famous nursery rhyme. I wonder how it would read now? There are some, no doubt, who would say Dumpty had it coming. You can't climb a wall that high with such a thin shell and expect to survive. Regardless, I would like to make an attempt at extending the ending to what we know to be true about Humpty Dumpty. After all, the ground isn't the end but just a beginning.

Humpty Dumpty sat on a wall,
Humpty Dumpty had a great fall.
All the king's horses and all the king's men
Couldn't put Humpty together again.

All the king's horses and all the king's men
Were just like Humpty—all filled up with sin.
But carpenter Jesus, with knowledge and skill
Repairs all who have fallen or taken a spill.

He was sent to fix those who fall from the wall,
Who fall from a height and have no hope at all.
He picks up the pieces all broken and cracked,
He was sent here to heal, redeem and buy back.

We all fall. Some fall farther than others. The velocity and ground do the damage. Some eggs crack, others break, but there is one thing for sure, Humpty Dumpty *can* be put back together again. I'm sorry to keep pushing it, but this nursery rhyme, as clever and cute as it may be, can have a different ending. The fall is only the first part of the story. If you are reading this, you may have experienced either the wall or the fall or both; but neither one has to be the end.

On the Wall

If you're on the wall, you can get off. It will take some dismantling and careful steps, but it is possible; it can be done.

In the Fall

You may be off the wall and in the middle of your fall. The ground is rushing toward you and you have little time to brace for impact. The concussion will be hard. It will be painful, you will crack and you might break. You will have scars and they will be visible. The ground is relentless. It does not budge, it does not absorb; it crushes and shatters. Rarely will God catch you in the fall. He's not being unkind or unloving. It's simply the first step in this "paradoxical process."

Standing Tall

Depending on what urban legend you believe about the great egg, there is hope. No, not from all the king's horses or all the king's men, but through loving friends, wise counselors and the power of the Holy Spirit.

In due time you will express the words written in Psalm 66:5-6,12: "Come and see what our God has done, what awesome miracles he performs for his people! He made a dry path through the Red Sea, and his people went across on foot. . . . We went through fire and flood. But you brought us to a place of great abundance."

"For though a righteous man falls seven times, he rises again" (Prov. 24:16, *NIV*). My dear friends, it's time to get up and continue your WALK. Continue your journey to a balanced life!

A New Day

You may find yourself in Bartimaeus's sandals today. You have answered Jesus and you have been healed. You were blind but now you see. You were broken but now you are repaired. Just like our son Cameron was physically *broken*, I (Craig) was *spiritually* broken. Cameron's healing is taking place over time, and I feel that is my spiritual path as well. It didn't take a day of counseling for us; it took months of counseling. Once Cameron saw 20/40, we didn't stop going to the eye doctor. We still go to several appointments each year to make sure he maintains his vision. We don't want him to regress with his vision or walk around with blurred vision the rest of his life. Clarity is what we want for him, and clarity is what we want for our family.

It's so easy to go back to the ways of the past. We have struggled with it while writing this book. We must remember that Bartimaeus *regained* his sight. He didn't *receive* it for the first time. He once saw clearly, and then became blind. After realizing what his life had become as a result of his blindness, he called out for healing at the right time and put his faith in the right person and was healed. His sight was *restored*. Jesus showed mercy to him because it is Jesus' nature to do so. "Because of the LORD's great love we are not consumed, for his compassions never fail. They are new every morning; great is your faithfulness" (Lam. 3:22-23, *NIV*).

While Mary and I were trying to STOP our life's SPIN and set a healthy PACE, God's mercies were there each morning. I can say that because we are writing about it today. Life was tough for several years. I might even go so far as to say, life was hell for several months. I spent years planting seeds of hurry, inattentiveness to my family and a lack of responsible care of my soul. When harvest time came, nothing good came from that crop. It's the law of the harvest. "Whatever you plant is what you'll harvest" (Gal. 6:7, *GOD'S WORD*).

We had to plant a new crop, which meant we needed to prepare the field, plant the right seeds, water, keep out bugs and pull the weeds from time to time. Preparing and planting is just the beginning. Things go right or wrong depending on how you care for the soil. From the time you plant until you harvest takes work and time. You don't just plant and walk away praying everything goes and grows well over time. I can tell you that our experience has been that a field left unattended gets overrun with weeds or consumed by bugs. I did the majority of the unhealthy planting in our family, and I followed that by being a poor farmer as well. After you plant the new seeds in your family field, it will take some time before you pick the fruit. This is also the law of the harvest. *It takes time to grow.*

When you plant the seeds of a healthy pace, awareness of your family's needs and healthy soul care, you will harvest a life consistent with what you planted. However, you will not see the product of the seeds until another season. I would prefer to have seen growth overnight and have a healthy harvest the next day, but that's not the law of the harvest. The law of the harvest says that what you plant is what you harvest; and the unwritten, unspoken law of the harvest is that you don't harvest in the season you plant; it takes time for the crop to grow. As we (the Jutilas) continue our journey to a balanced life, we have found that the law of the harvest with family is more on line with months or years, not weeks. It's a slow-growing plant, but it responds well to the proper care.

15

LOOK FORWARD

---

*A man travels the world in search of what he needs
and returns home to find it.*

GEORGE EDWARD MOORE
(ENGLISH PHILOSOPHER)

Reaching Forward

As our family continues to move forward, we must look well beyond each daily step. There's a bigger picture on the horizon. We have taken Paul's approach when he says, "No, dear brothers and sisters, I am still not all I should be, but I am focusing all my energies on this one thing: Forgetting the past and looking forward to what lies ahead" (Phil. 3:13). Looking ahead helps us plan our calendar, see the bigger picture and take advantage of the time we have together. In the past, we put things on the calendar but never really had a "looking forward" awareness about us. We, especially me (Craig), had a more reactionary take on life. Now that we maintain a heads-up approach to our family life, things are clearer, and we can see life in context with some long-range perspective.

We have come to take Ephesians 5:15-17 as our "looking forward family focus": "So be careful how you live, not as fools but as those who are wise. Make the most of every opportunity for doing good in these evil days. Don't act thoughtlessly, but try to understand what the Lord wants you to do." The words "Make the most of every opportunity" reverberate in my mind. What opportunities can Mary and I take advantage of in our future? How can we creatively plan opportunities to breathe life and energy into our family? What if we have blown opportunities in the past? That's one question that can haunt me if I let it. When I begin to look back, I have to remember Paul's words in Philippians and look forward and press on. The enemy of our souls wants us to look back with regret. Our heavenly father wants us to look ahead with hope and take advantage of the opportunities that are in front of us.

It's interesting to see how the words "Make the most of every opportunity" in the *New Living Translation* were originally used. The six words in the original text mean "redeeming the time" or "buying the time." Of course, we all understand that it's impossible to get more time or go somewhere to buy more time. The question isn't, "Do we have enough time in our day?" The questions are, "What are we doing with the time we have?" and "Are we taking advantage of the time we have?" If we miss an opportunity, we can't get it back. Time keeps moving on.

The thought conveyed in Ephesians 5:16 originally came years ago with merchants that would take advantage of the right season when selling their merchandise to get the most money for their products. A savvy businessperson would take this advantage in order to make a better profit. For the merchant as a consumer, making the most of their time meant looking for and taking advantage of the best possible price among other merchants selling their products.[1] Today, a merchant or consumer looks for a great sale by looking through catalogs, newspapers and Internet sites for the best price. After they have compared the items and prices, they make a wise purchase using the best deal they can find. They have then taken advantage of the opportunity. They have made the most of their time. They were diligent, resourceful and aware.

We are encouraged to take the same attitude with our time. We aren't supposed to let time pass by. We are supposed to take advantage of our time and look for opportunities. We make the most of our time by spending it wisely. We buy up moments in our family life that others might throw away. You can't get the time back that you have already spent. I'm sure all of us have made poor purchases in our past, with both our money and our time. Does anyone own a set of steak knives, a juicer or another late-night spontaneous purchase you would like to chalk up to a moment of weak judgment?

We need to buy up every available moment and not let it slip by. We should leverage each opportunity and not let it get away from us. There is a skillfulness and shrewdness that comes with making the most of your time. It takes effort to discern where the opportunities are and then spend time accordingly.

The unique thing about a sale is that it doesn't last long. Sales are there for a brief moment, and you either take advantage of them or let them pass. If we are to make the most of our time, we need to make the most of it now. Not tomorrow, not when you finish school, not when you achieve a certain financial status. Now.

As our story reflects, Mary and I missed many opportunities for making the most of the time. I (Craig) made the choice to let the opportunities pass in the early years of our family. We can regret the past or remedy the future. Let's remedy the future. Let's make changes now to take advantage of the time we have left. We understand that we are still not as we should be, but we are focusing all of our energy on one thing: forgetting the past and looking forward to what's ahead. We aren't chained to our past. We've learned from it and moved on.

Unfortunately, we can't just sit back and expect the *good deals* in life to come to us. We must do the looking and comparing to find the most suitable way to make the most of our time with our family. That will mean saying no to other *good deals*, other opportunities, in favor of the *best* opportunity. We can only do this by reaching forward and looking ahead, not looking back. When you look back at a sale you missed, you may say, "Now that I look back, I wish I could have . . ." or "I wish I would have . . ." Vision is pretty clear when you look back; hindsight is always 20/20. It's when you look ahead that life can get a little fuzzy; but that's where our faith comes in. We ask God for the wisdom necessary to make the most of our time and take advantage of every opportunity.

If we don't take advantage of our time, it slowly drifts away just like a leaf on a slow-moving stream. If we are passive with our time, it simply passes by. Time doesn't stop while you try to decide how to take advantage of it. Time is relentless that way. Taking advantage of each opportunity requires a certain diligence from each one of us. If we don't take time by the hand it will usually take us by the wrist just like the song says: "Another turning point, a fork stuck in the road. Time grabs you by the wrist, directs you where to go."[2] We must command our calendar and control our time or it will fade away or, worse, control us.

Start at Home

How well do you really know your family? I bet you think you know them really well. Tell me, what is your spouse's love language—what speaks love to him or her? Do you know each of your children's love languages? If you want them to feel your love, this is an important thing to know. My (Mary's) love languages are acts of service, and gifts. It thrills me when someone jumps in and helps me, whether it's helping make dinner or doing a bigger task, like washing my Mini Cooper. I especially love it when Craig comes to my school at the beginning of each year and helps me put up my bulletin boards. He takes the time to get the paper straight and the wrinkles out and can reach places that I can't reach, even with a ladder! Being surprised with a small gift, like a latte or a flower, goes a long way with me too. I may have gotten this love language from my mom, since she is one to always show up with a little gift.

I can remember when Mom and I worked for the same company when I was in college. Sometimes I would come into the office and find a little gift on my desk with a note from her. When the boys were young, she was constantly picking up a toy train or car to surprise them with. And when Karimy came along, she was just as thrilled as I was to have a little girl to shop and sew for. Mom embroidered everything she could with Karimy's name, made beautiful bows for her hair and surprised her with doll clothes she had made. This is how she *loves* others.

I have found out that Craig's love language is *not* gifts. I still love to buy him little things, like his favorite cookies from Trader Joe's, but this doesn't *show* him love like it does me. His primary love language is words of affirmation. Leaving a card or a note for him; telling him that I love him, appreciate him or think he is awesome is how I *show* him that I love him. His other love language is touch. It means a lot to him when I hold his hand, scratch his back and rub his head. This is his other love language and a hard one for me to demonstrate on days when I am keeping too hectic a pace. (It sure would be easier to just buy him a little gift!)

This love language idea translates to the kids as well. All three of our kids have a different love language. If you don't know what your spouse or your child's love language is, there are some excellent books and websites with different love language assessments.[3]

I asked each of our kids to take the test to determine their love language and was surprised to find out the results. Karimy is also an "acts of service" person, which explains why she so often offers to help me in the kitchen and gets very upset when someone can't or won't help her. She is also great at helping her brothers when they "let" her clean their rooms. She is not a "physical touch" person and is my one child that I have to ask to get a hug or a kiss. Seeing her love language results helped me realize this and not take it personally. We recommend that all families take the time to learn about each other's love languages. With just a little effort pointed in the right direction, you can really show your family that you love them in a way they will understand.

You Can Go Again

We have a tradition at dinnertime that we started when the boys were little. It doesn't cost any money. It doesn't take any planning ahead. It's simple. It's easy. But it's a *big* deal to our kids. Are you ready for this? It's a red plate we put at someone's place setting that says, "You are special today." Whoever gets the red plate is the center of attention at the dinner table.

We all take a turn to tell that person why he or she is special. Our rules are simple; you can't compliment the person on something he or she is wearing. It needs to be something the person did that was kind or thoughtful or meant a lot to someone else in the family. Once when Karimy was in kindergarten, after everyone had gone around and told her why she was special, she said, "You can go again, if you want to. It's okay." We all had a great big laugh, but it struck me (Mary) how much this little family ritual meant to her and how much she needed to be affirmed by us. She had a huge need for love, as we all do. Love needs to start in the home, with mom and dad loving each other first of all, and then loving the kids and the kids loving each other. Easier said than done, right?

A few years ago, we stumbled upon a creative way to affirm each other. I had put a large sticky-backed poster on the wall for the ladies' Bible study group that met at our house on Thursday nights. I had written a question on it and left a jar full of markers so the ladies could write their answers on the poster. The question simply was, "What is love?"

A few days after the Bible study, I noticed that the kids had begun to write their answers to the question on the paper as well. And so it was that I began to leave the poster up in the front hallway so the kids could add to it. When Alec and Cameron's birthday arrived, I wrote in the middle of one large poster, "What we love about Alec" and then on a separate one, "What we love about Cameron." Soon little doodles and words began popping up on both the posters as family members walked by and listed things they appreciated about them. I laughed when I caught Cameron writing on his own poster "Cool" and "Awesome" when he thought no one was looking.

When friends came by, they added to it, and after a few weeks there was no room left. Now those posters were *keepers*! We moved them upstairs to each of their rooms where they could be reminded daily of how much they are loved and appreciated by others. Talk about a confidence booster! When my birthday rolled around a few months later, my sweet daughter, all on her own, found the poster paper and made a sign for me that read, "Why we love Mom." I'll be honest with you. It really encouraged me.

Marking the special occasions, like birthdays and anniversaries, is a perfect way to show someone in your family how much you value them. Don't celebrate it on another day. Celebrate it on *their* day. After all, it only comes once a year and it is *their day!* So what can you do to show your family members they are loved, special and valued? What about taking the day off of work to spend it with them? How about showing up at your kid's school with their favorite burger and fries and then sitting down to eat it with them? Or maybe you could send flowers to your wife on the anniversary of your first date. (Craig did that for me, and you should have seen the gals in the front office . . . boy, were they impressed!)

You don't have to spend extra money to make someone's day. My mom used to ask each of us kids what we would like for dinner and she would cook that for us. It didn't matter if anyone else in the family liked it or wanted to eat it that night. It was our special day and it was our turn to choose. I loved that part of my birthday. We also were given a pardon on doing work of any kind on our birthday. We didn't even have to clear our plate or clean our room! That was enough to make my day right there. No chores? I'll take that any day!

Planning ahead is *huge*. So don't ask your spouse on the day of his or her birthday or on your anniversary either of these questions: "What do you want to do today?" or "What would you like for your birthday/anniversary?" That's a good way to *ruin* their day. They will probably answer "Nothing," since it is obvious that that is what you have done up to this point. Lack of planning conveys to your spouse that he or she is not valuable enough for you to prioritize his/her special day. Ask your spouse if he or she wants a party, and then plan a party if the answer is yes. Guys, go buy paper goods with little cupcakes or flowers on them. Order his or her favorite cake, pie or ice cream cake. Or make a cake! Invite their friends over to celebrate and play board games, if they are an extrovert and enjoy hanging out with people. It's a big deal to them. Take this opportunity to shower them with your love and appreciation. Trust me, you will be glad you did. Especially when *your* birthday rolls around.

Another way to love your family is to spend dinnertime with them. It doesn't matter if you are serving Chef Boyardee or Filet Mignon for dinner. It will just be better if you are *there*. We have found that eating together can be a difficult thing to schedule and a difficult thing to manage, but the rewards are worth it. In fact, we have even had feedback from other families that began to have regular dinners together. They told us that it was downright painful at the beginning. We heard stories of arguing at the table, complaining from teenagers and some completely silent meal times. It will take some time for everyone to adjust to this new "normal" of eating dinner together. But it is worth it if you stick with the plan and make mealtimes a family time.

One thing that might help you get through those awkward dinner times is planning some purposeful conversations at the table. Besides the red plate time, we go around and share "highs" and "lows" of our day with each other. I have heard of other people calling this "roses" and "thorns." Make up your own name for it if you want, but I encourage you to try it. You will learn a lot about your family. This is a great way to find out what is going on in your kids' lives at school and at your spouse's job. This is a time when they are likely to open up and share with you what really bothers them and what really excites them.

While on vacation in Carmel, California, one year, we found a really cool resource called Table Topics for Families. It's a little box of questions or conversation starters to use with your kids. Sometimes we pull that out and take turns answering the questions in the box. We also found some that were made just for couples and just for families with teens. Purposeful communication around the table sure beats watching television, arguing or sitting there in silence. Make your dinnertime a time when you can connect and talk about feelings, hopes and dreams as a couple or as a family. Use this time to build into your children spiritually. Some families even do a short devotional after dinner and spend time praying together.

We have also learned that loving our kids means showing up for their sports events, piano recitals, awards at school, parent-teacher conferences (both parents if at all possible), the school open house . . . you get the idea. Showing up says that you value them and what they are involved in. You are proud of them. You love them.

No one can take your place at these venues and events. No one. Be there when they need you. Be there and be "presently engaged" when you are there. In other words, as hard as it is, don't use your phone, your iPad, your computer or other electronic device when you are "showing up" for them. Because that isn't really showing up, is it? (Smile.) That is multitasking, like we talked about in chapter 5, which isn't good for you or for them.

I know how hard that is to do. I (Mary) struggle with this still. It is hard for me to go to a basketball game and not get on my phone during halftime. Sometimes it is hard for me to attend an all-day swim meet and not feel like I am wasting my Saturday. This is easier for some people than for others. But being a recovering adrenaline addict, multi-tasker and workaholic makes it a very tough thing for me. But it is the right thing to do because it requires me to simply *be*. I am the only mom my kids have. And I want to be an attentive, loving mom who can pause and enjoy my kids along life's journey.

16

KEEP
PERSPECTIVE

You can't turn back the clock. But you can wind it up again.
BONNIE PRUDDEN

Crisis Comes, and Sometimes We Linger

I (Craig) was the kid who touched the stove to see if it was hot. For the most part, I have made the most significant changes in my life as a result of hurting enough that I had to make a change. I can remember my mom's words to me as I was growing up when I was either about to make a dumb choice, was in the process of making a dumb choice or had already made one. She would say, "You know better than that!" Well, yes, I did know better than that. So why make the dumb choices?

I finally found the answer: It's not me making the bad choices. Take a look at Romans 7:15-17: "I don't understand myself at all, for I really want to do what is right, but I don't do it. Instead, I do the very thing I hate. I know perfectly well that what I am doing is wrong, and my bad conscience shows that I agree that the law is good. But I can't help myself, because it is sin inside me that makes me do these evil things." Apparently, Paul was having the same issue. In fact, aren't we all having the same issue? This passage is not the "let's blame the bad nature so we have no responsibility" passage. Paul is letting us know that if we are in Christ, we are not making the bad choices; the sin inside us is.

Sometimes crisis comes as a result of our own SPIN and sometimes God allows crisis into our life through no fault of our own. When we make choices that are not consistent with God's plan for us, there are consequences to those choices, and they vary in severity. We have all felt the consequences of our actions, both good and bad. But the long-term outcome of those bad decisions can be turned into God's glory. The goal is to learn, and live more like Christ: more love, more forgiveness, more grace and more mercy to others.

There are situations in life that just happen. You did not choose them; they chose you. God allowed a difficult and trying circumstance into your life. You didn't deserve it; you didn't ask for it; it just happened. When something comes into your life that is difficult, disturbing or decidedly despicable, rest assured that God knew it was coming. "Dear brothers and sisters, whenever trouble comes your way, let it be an opportunity for joy. For when your faith is tested, your endurance has a chance to grow" (Jas. 1:2-3). "Whenever" is the word, not "if." God allows these things into our life to give us endurance, to mature us, to make us and mold us to be more like Him.

Sitting next to our son in the recovery room of Jules Stein Eye Institute at UCLA Medical Center is an experience we have lived several times over. Mary and I aren't strangers to this facility, and neither is Cameron.

As a father sitting at the foot of his son's hospital bed, I can honestly tell you that I don't really care too much how he got here. I am more interested in his recovery and his future health. In Cameron's case, his choices did not put him here. An unfortunate accident put him here. Under God's care? Yes. Did God put him here? No. Did God allow him to be here? Yes.

What if Cameron had been older and was making careless choices with his life—maybe a sort of prodigal son experience where he ventured out and lived a lifestyle in complete denial of his family? Would I sit at the foot of his hospital bed ready with a lecture or ready with grace and mercy when he awakes? I would think the story of the prodigal son would give us some insight on how we are to act as parents. Isn't it a picture of our heavenly father and how He deals with us? Our Father is not accusatory by nature. If He were, He wouldn't have sent His only Son to die on a cross to redeem us, to buy us back. He would have simply pointed a finger and said, "I told you so."

Whether your past, present or future crisis could be described as self-inflicted or God-allowed, you can have the same outcome; and that is to be more like Him in your everyday life. Even though crisis will come to each one of us, we don't have to linger in it. God will keep us in the middle of the storm for as long as necessary, but not a minute longer, to mature us. Hope in this truth gets you through and moves you on to the other side. Don't live in the past. Learn from it and move on.

Called to the Other Side

The choices I (Craig) made with my time and energy put our family boat in the middle of a storm. Yes, God *allowed* us to be there, but I *put* us there. I have to be honest and assume responsibility for how I lived my life and how my life choices affected my whole family and close friends. There were times when I wished I was in the boat all by myself, left to feel the pain and suffer the consequences of my SPIN alone; but I wasn't. Most of a person's unhealthy choices and decisions end up affecting others, and usually that means those we love the most. My whole family was in the boat with me. We were all in the middle of the storm.

The Gospel of Mark tells a story about just such a time when a few guys were caught in a boat out in the middle of a storm. This story has some important reminders for us as we face storms in our own lives today.

After the feeding of the five thousand, "Jesus made His disciples get into the boat and go ahead of Him *to the other side* to Bethsaida, while He Himself was sending the crowd away" (Mark 6:45, *NASB*, emphasis added). I can't tell you how many times I have read this verse over the years and missed this principle every time. My mind always moves forward in this story to where Jesus is walking on the water and Peter jumps out and starts to sink. I never really paid close attention to the words of verse 45. Jesus' plan for His disciples was to send them to the other side, not keep them in the middle.

My family and I spent the better part of two years in the *middle* of the storm and couldn't see the other side, never mind trying to get there. At this point in our life, we were just trying to stay in the boat. It seemed like life was capsizing and our only option was to drown under life's crashing waves.

Regardless of how you got into the middle of the storm, there are choices you can make to get to the other side. If you paddled into it, God can help you out of it. There will be some lessons learned—perhaps painful ones—but you can get to the other side.

Jesus' intention for His disciples was to go *across* the lake, not drown in the middle of it. Jesus never calls us to the middle of the storm. He always calls us to the other side. The middle of the storm is a temporary location, not a permanent address. We are simply passing through.

As Jesus was sitting on the side of the hill that late afternoon, "He saw that they [His disciples] were in serious trouble, rowing hard and struggling against the wind and waves" (Mark 6:48). Jesus is sitting on shore and He is witnessing the disciples in the middle of the storm. They are frightened and fatigued, but He doesn't run out to rescue them. In fact, He walks. He could see the storm brewing. He could see His disciples in distress. He knew they were in trouble, but He doesn't run or jump to save them. He walks. Why? He has a plan for them in the middle of the storm.

Have there been times in your life when you felt that Jesus wasn't there with you in the middle of the storm? We have. It's hard to get our feelings to follow the facts, but we know Jesus is there, we know we are under His watchful eye. But sometimes my feelings are disconnected from my head and it feels like He isn't there when He is. Jesus doesn't call us to the middle of the storm alone; at the right time, He will walk by.

There have been times in our journey when we felt as if God was not there or He needed to move more quickly. We have felt like we needed to tie a knot at the end of the rope just to hang on. We have experienced storms that were brought on by our own choices, and we have experienced the storms life has simply blown our way. Though we may feel at times like God is not there, He is. We cannot mistake His walking as disinterest or lack of love. Nothing escapes God's watchful eye. From the disciples in the boat to your life in crisis, everything is played out under the clear view of a loving God.

Sometimes it *feels* like He is not there and sometimes it also *feels* like He isn't watching, but He is. He may not run out and rescue you out there in the middle. The middle is part of His plan for each of us. It's where we learn faith and we exercise hope. He has a plan for us in the middle: "They are plans for good and not for disaster, to give you a future and a hope" (Jer. 29:11). Strong character is forged in the middle of the storm, not on the safety of the shore.

Jesus didn't run to the rescue; He walked. "About three o'clock in the morning he came to them, walking on the water" (Mark 6:48). Jesus' timing is never off, even by a second. Sure, there have been times when we felt He needed to move and He didn't; but when we are in the middle of the storm, we lose awareness of time. Crisis does that to us. We go into fight-or-flight mode; and in those moments, who cares about the other side? We are just trying to survive the storm! Our Lord always sees the other side.

The words that really catch my attention in this story are the last few words of verse 48. Picture the moment. There's a storm in the middle of the lake. The disciples are frightened for their life. Jesus sees this and starts walking on the water toward the boat, and then the final words of this verse: "He started to go past them" (Mark 6:48).

He wasn't walking to them; He was walking by them. The *New American Standard* version says, "He intended to pass by them." Why would Jesus start to go past the disciples? Why would He get all the way out to them and go on by? Maybe Jesus was looking for something. Maybe He was waiting for something. Maybe He wanted His disciples to recognize He was right there with them in the middle of the storm. Maybe He wanted His disciples to look to Him for salvation from the storm or at least take comfort in His presence.

Once the disciples realized it was Jesus, Peter got it right. Most of what we read about Peter is the sinking part, but at least he got out of the boat. He experienced the supernatural power that faith brings. So did Bartimaeus, for that matter. The others may have had faith, but they didn't exercise it. Jesus wants us to call out to Him from the middle of the storm. He wants us to exercise our faith and rely on the hope He provides.

Mary and I had to make a choice to focus on our journey and on our walk, not on the wind and the waves. The wind is fierce and the waves can be devastating. Like the song "Voice of Truth" says, "The waves they keep on telling me time and time again, 'Boy, you'll never win!' You'll never win! But the voice of truth tells me a different story."[1] The voice of truth says you are created in God's image. The voice of truth says don't be afraid. The voice of truth says nothing can separate you from God's love. The voice of truth says the middle is not our destination, it's just a necessary delay en route to the other side.

There Is Always Hope

In the middle of all things SPIN, we woke up to find our beloved family cat laying in pain on our kitchen floor. We gathered the kids, picked up the cat and hurried to the vet where she later died. It was emotional chaos and a painful family moment that day. Not even a week later, I received a phone call from my dad. He told me he had just returned from the doctor where they told him he had cancer. Surgery, radiation and chemotherapy were now on his horizon. The weight of life seemed too heavy to lift and one day Mary and I fell under the weight. In the corner of our bedroom we both collapsed into a puddle of tears, clutching each other and wondering what was next.

The words came out of the speakers in our home: "And though my heart is torn, I will praise You in this storm."[2] God was speaking to us in our tearful puddle, saying, "I am here." We were talking back: "God, please let it stop." What do you do in that moment? Maybe the better question is, what *can* you do in that moment?

"He comforts us in all our troubles so that we can comfort others. When others are troubled, we will be able to give them the same comfort God has given us" (2 Cor. 1:4). We don't know what our future holds, but we do know who holds our future, and that's what keeps us moving. We look forward, not back; to what's next, not to what has happened. Hope keeps us moving forward when life wants to hold us down.

God will never waste a hurt or a healing you have experienced. He wants you to share your stories of pain and progress so that others can be encouraged, so that others may have hope. He comforts us, then we comfort others, and on and on it goes. The pressure we endure helps us understand the pain others experience. We are all in this together, and if one of us is hurting and feeling like there's no way out, then those who have been through the same tunnel can give some wisdom to those in the middle. Don't give up! Hang in there! Keep moving! Keep believing, and "without wavering, let us hold tightly to the hope we say we have, for God can be trusted to keep his promise" (Heb. 10:23).

God promises we will have crisis, but it doesn't linger. God promises the middle but points us to the shore. And after we have "suffered a little while, he will restore, support, and strengthen you, and he will place you on a firm foundation" (1 Pet. 5:10). When you are on that firm foundation, you will reach out to offer hope to those around you.

As we near the end of this book, you may be at the beginning of difficulty. Maybe you feel like you have lived a hectic life and want some health. Maybe you want to journey with someone who has been there and knows the right path to take. No matter where life has you in this moment, keep your perspective. God is a miracle worker and can reverse the out-of-balance life you have been living and restore the relationships with those you have hurt the most. "I will repay you for the years the locusts have eaten" (Joel 2:25, *NIV*).

There is an interesting phenomenon that occurs every day along the Saint John River in Saint John, New Brunswick. The river is the longest river in Atlantic Canada, with a length of 418 miles. The river empties into the Bay of Fundy located between Maine and Nova Scotia. The most interesting thing about this river is a phenomenon called the Reversing Falls, which is caused by the high tides of the Bay of Fundy.

Each day the river flows downstream and into the bay. The Bay of Fundy at low tide is about 14 feet lower than the natural level of the river, which allows the river to empty into the bay. But what would happen if the tide rose above 14 feet? Wouldn't it push the river in the opposite direction? The answer is yes. And that's what happens every day along the Saint John River. When high tide rolls in, the bay begins to rise and eventually interrupts the flow of the river. Once the bay fills to the height at which the river is flowing, the river stops moving and lays perfectly calm. Those who travel the river call this time "slack tide," and it's the only time during the day that boats can safely travel on the river. As high tide continues to fill the bay, it actually begins to push the river in the opposite direction. The river reverses its flow. The force of the rising tide is so strong that rapids actually develop in the opposite direction. High tide peaks at nearly 14 feet higher than the flow of the river, causing the reversing rapids.[3]

The unusual nature of the Saint John River is a great illustration for our busy, hectic and out-of-balance lives. We need to keep a proper perspective, push the pause button, praise God, party, have fun, enjoy life and practice healthy soul care. Each one of these things raises the level of the bay in our lives. When our life begins to *rise up* with healthy habits and the power of God, our past pain can reverse. Like reversing rapids, out-of-balance living finds a healthy pace; relationships return to intimacy and marriages heal.

CONCLUSION

No matter what situation you find yourself in, you always have a future, and it's always filled with hope, even when you know life storms are coming. Mary and I made a decision to put one foot in front of the other and slowly begin to walk out of the stormy life we were living. Pain taught us that. I wish it was quicker and easier, but it isn't and it wasn't. It was long and painful. If you must put a timeline on it, we would say three years. Not three years to "get it right"; we still haven't done that. No, three years from pain to the point of Understanding SPIN, Learning STOP, Setting PACE and our current WALK.

We have a new perspective on our journey that would not be the same without the storms that battered our boat. We have shared part of our journey with you to give you hope. Your situation may be better than ours, or it may be worse. But God is the same. He promises that His mercies are new every morning and that His faithfulness is great. We *know* that to be true. We have lived it. We have experienced God's grace, mercy, compassion, forgiveness, healing, redemption and restoration. Sometimes the storms are strong and the winds push us off the road, and that's when someone comes along to help us up so that we can continue the journey. It is our hope and prayer that this book will do that for you—help you up and set you on your journey. We would love to meet you and encourage you as we travel together to a healthier and more balanced life.

Until then,

Craig and Mary
www.hectictohealthy.com/journey

"Though you have made me see troubles, many and bitter, you will restore my life again; from the depths of the earth you will again bring me up" (Ps. 71:20, *NIV*).

ENDNOTES

Chapter 1: Seasons

1. Dictionary.com, "Definition of Addiction," http://dictionary.reference.com/browse/addiction (accessed August 2011).

Chapter 3: Isolation

1. Casting Crowns, "Stained Glass Masquerade" (Brentwood, TN: Reunion Records, 2005). http://castingcrowns.com/node/631.

Chapter 4: Neglect

1. Gordon MacDonald, *Ordering Your Private World* (Nashville, TN: Thomas Nelson Publishers), p. 13.

Chapter 6: Think Ahead

1. Dr. Archibald D. Hart, *Adrenaline and Stress* (Nashville, TN: Thomas Nelson Publishers, 1995), p. 82.
2. Phyllis Korkki, "When Hard Work Becomes Overwork," *New York Times*, October 21, 2007. http://tiny.cc/3vk34 (accessed August 2011).
3. Neil Osterweil, "Are You a Workaholic?," WebMD, 2008. http://www.webmd.com/balance/guide/are-you-a-workaholic (accessed August 2011).
4. "Definition of Eustress," Dictionary.com. http://dictionary.reference.com/browse/eustress (accessed August 2011).
5. Daniel J. DeNoon, "Long Hours Up High Blood Pressure Risk," WebMD, August 28, 2006. http://tinyurl.com/yrscjt (accessed August 2011).

Chapter 7: Open Up

1. Peter Berg, director, *The Kingdom* (Universal City, CA: Universal Pictures, 2007).

Chapter 8: Pause Often

1. Roy Adams, "Keeping The Sabbath," *Adventist Review* http://www.adventistreview.org/article.php?id=1207 (accessed September 2011).
2. *Webster's Revised Unabridged Dictionary,* 1913, "Sabbath."
3. Jacquelyn Smith, "The Companies Doing the Most to Make Their Employees Happier," *Forbes,* August 29, 2011, http://www.forbes.com/sites/jacquelynsmith/2011/08/29/the-companies-doing-the-most-to-make-their-employees-happier/ (accessed September 2011).

Chapter 9: Practice Soul Care

1. Mercy Me, "Hold Fast," (New York: Sony, 2006). http://www.lyricsdomain.com/13/mercy_me/hold_fast.html (accessed September 2011).
2. Casting Crowns, "Praise You in This Storm" (Brentwood, TN: Reunion, 2005). http://www.lyricsdomain.com/3/casting_crowns/praise_you_in_this_storm.html (accessed September 2011).
3. Mercy Me, "My Heart Will Fly" (New York: Sony, 2007). http://www.lyricsdomain.com/13/mercy_me/my_heart_will_fly.html (accessed September 2011).
4. Adam Clarke, *Commentary on the Bible,* 1831. http://clarke.biblecommenter.com/james/4.htm (accessed September 2011).

Chapter 10: Act Accordingly

1. Rebecca Ray, Janet C. Gormick and John Schmitt, "Parental Leave Policies in 21 Countries—Assessing Generosity and Gender Equality," Center for Economic and Policy Research, Washington D.C., September 2008, pp. 2-3.

Chapter 11: Come Together
1. John and Stasi Eldredge, *Captivating: Unveiling the Mystery of a Woman's Soul* (Nashville, TN: Thomas Nelson Inc., 2005).
2. Ibid.

Chapter 12: Enjoy Life
1. C. S. Lewis, *Letters to an American Lady* (Grand Rapids, MI: Eerdman's, 1975), p. 53.
2. Steve Ayan, "Laughing Matters," *Scientific American Mind*, May 2009, p. 25.

Chapter 13: Watch Out
1. C. S. Lewis, *The Screwtape Letters* (West Chicago, IL: Lord and King Associates, Inc.), p. 29.
2. Neil T. Anderson, *The Bondage Breaker* (Eugene, OR: Harvest House Publishers, 2000), p. 224.
3. Adam Clarke, *Clarke's Commentary on the Bible*. http://clarke.biblecommenter.com/job/42.htm (accessed September 2011).
4. Matthew Henry, *Matthew Henry's Concise Commentary on the Bible*. http://mhc.biblecommenter.com/job/42.htm (accessed September 2011).

Chapter 14: Answer Him
1. Joseph Ritson, *Gammer Gurton's Garland: Or, the Nursery Parnassus; a Choice Collection of Pretty Songs and Verses, for the Amusement of All Little Good Children Who Can Neither Read Nor Run* (London: Harding and Wright, 1810), p. 36.
2. I. Opie and P. Opie, *The Oxford Dictionary of Nursery Rhymes* (Oxford: Oxford University Press, 1951, 1997), pp. 213-215.
3. "Paradox," Online Etymology Dictionary. http://www.etymonline.com/index.php?search=paradox&searchmode=none.

Chapter 15: Look Forward
1. Adam Clarke, *Commentary on the Bible*, 1831. http://clarke.biblecommenter.com/ephesians/5.htm (accessed September 2011).
2. Green Day, "Time of Your Life," (Burbank CA: Reprise Records, 1997). http://www.lyricsdomain.com/7/green_day/time_of_your_life_good_riddance.html.
3. Dr. Gary Chapman, *The 5 Love Languages* (Chicago, IL: Northfield Publishing, 2010). http://www.5lovelanguages.com/assessments/love (accessed September 2011).

Chapter 16: Keep Perspective
1. Casting Crowns, "Voice of Truth" (Brentwood, TN: Reunion Records, 2003). http://castingcrowns.com/node/629.
2. Casting Crowns, "Life Song" (Brentwood, TN: Reunion Records, 2003). http://casting crowns.com/node/629.
3. "Reversing Falls," New-Brunswick.net. http://new-brunswick.net/Saint_John/reversingfalls/reversing.html (accessed September 2011).

RECOMMENDED READING

Anderson, Neil. *The Bondage Breaker*. Eugene, OR: Harvest House Publishers, 2006.

Arbinger Institute. *Leadership and Self Deception: Getting Out of the Box*. San Francisco, CA: Berrett-Koehler Publishers, Inc, 2010.

Eldredge, John and Stasi. *Captivating: Unveiling the Mystery of a Woman's Soul*. Nashville, TN: Thomas Nelson, 2011.

Hart, Archibald D. *Adrenaline and Stress: The Exciting New Breakthrough that Helps You Overcome Stress Damage*. Nashville, TN: Thomas Nelson, 1995.

———. *Thrilled to Death: How the Endless Pursuit of Pleasure Is Leaving Us Numb*. Nashville, TN: Thomas Nelson, 2007.

Lencioni, Patrick. *The Three Big Questions for a Frantic Family: A Leadership Fable About Restoring Sanity to the Most Important Organization in Your Life*. San Francisco, CA: Jossey-Bass, 2008.

MacDonald, Gordon. *Ordering Your Private World*. Nashville, TN: Thomas Nelson, 2007.

Scazzero, Peter. *Emotionally Healthy Spirituality: Unleash a Revolution in Your Life in Christ*. Nashville, TN: Thomas Nelson, 2011.

ACKNOWLEDGMENTS

We want to thank our "Balance Board," as we affectionately refer to them. These are our friends and family who walked with us through our stormy season and continue to remind us of the importance of *being* instead of *doing*. Thank you for taking the time to read our words and give honest feedback. Thank you for encouraging us to keep writing and for lifting us up in prayer. We appreciate you more than you know. We love you.

Gordon and Jill Bourns
Jill Catuara
Gregg and Janine Farah
Jeff and Sherry Joyner
Chris and Dawn Lewis
Dr. Jim Mastellar
Ed and Dolly McGuigan
Joe and Janet Moser
Oran and Laura Pentz
Debbie Reed